8 WEEKS TO LONGER HAIR!

8 WEEKS TO LONGER HAIR!

A Guide for the Afro-Caribbean Woman. Discover Your Hair's Growth Potential!

Lola Akingbola

www.lolascurls.com

Starting out on a journey is good in and of itself, but what really sets it apart and increases the chances of your success is *your focus and planning*. This book simply gives you steps to help ensure you are still working towards your hair care goals daily and weekly. Consistency is the key. As you continue to repeat these techniques, they will become a habit for you—it takes 60 days (eight weeks) for something to become a habit. Take it one day at a time and you will get there!

Library of Congress Control Number: 2013911145
ISBN: Hardcover   978-1-4836-5721-9
               Softcover   978-1-4836-5720-2
               Ebook   978-1-4836-5722-6

Rev. date: 07/31/2013

To order additional copies of this book, contact:
Xlibris LLC
0-800-056-3182
www.xlibrispublishing.co.uk
Orders@xlibrispublishing.co.uk
305943

CONTENTS

Introduction

This is not just another hair care book. This is 'the book' to help you transform your hair.

It is a well-known fact that new habits take 60 days to become ingrained in our routines. That is exactly why I am taking you on the first 60 days of your new hair journey.

This is not a book to tell you a bunch of facts about hair. It is not a book to preach new techniques or throw new products at you. It is definitely not a book to show you my long hair and give you empty promises about your hair's growth!

The purpose of this book is to inform, inspire, and encourage you to get the hair you want in the next 8 weeks. I do not claim that your hair will be down to your butt in 8 weeks. Let's stay in the realm of reality here. I do promise that if you take the steps at the end of each chapter, you *will* achieve at least an inch of hair growth, accompanied by thicker hair, stronger strands, and smoother hair. An inch of growth every two months from then, once these new techniques become your hair habits, adds up quite quickly! 2 inches can be enough to make your hair reach past your shoulders on the way to reaching your bra strap.

Overleaf is a chart of hair lengths that you will become quite familiar with. The important thing is to remember to set realistic goals for your hair. You should also set realistic times to reach these goals. The second thing I want you to remember is that these techniques are *focussed on achieving hair health*. This is how I started my journey. *Any practice geared towards hair health will inevitably lead to hair growth through length retention.* I want you to focus on hair health first, and you will reap rewards in length as I have.

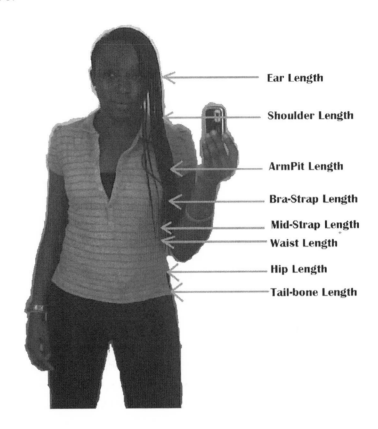

Ear Length

Shoulder Length

ArmPit Length

Bra-Strap Length

Mid-Strap Length

Waist Length

Hip Length

Tail-bone Length

Each chapter will be a lesson for the week. Each week, I will introduce one of the eight important changes to my hair routine that really took my hair growth to the next level. I will also debunk a hair myth for each chapter, as I feel that holding on to false notions about our hair always threatens to overwhelm our newfound knowledge.

I am going to start with a brief pictorial history of my hair journey over the last 4 years. Then I am going to launch into our first week. Feel free to read ahead for the coming week(s) as you like. I encourage that eagerness to get started on the journey to the hair you always wanted.

My Hair History—Part One

I am a Nigerian—born and raised—with both parents being fully Nigerian and I can count back to around 4 generations of Nigerian ancestors on both sides. I have fine coily, wiry strands of hair, but I have a lot of them! I had relaxed hair for almost 20 years of my life. Only in the last 2 years of relaxing my hair did I know how to truly manage my hair in that state. Before my hair journey, my hair never got past my shoulders—*shoulder length*—at its longest.

As it thrived, I wanted more of a challenge. I decided to grow out my relaxer *and* grow my hair to its longest length yet—waist length. When I surpassed that goal, I grew it to hip length. This was just before I ended my transition to natural hair. With this haircut, my hair was back to touching my bra strap. It is still growing!

I will tell you now, many people told me my hair would never get that long. Here's another secret, I had prayed for waist-length hair for *4 years* before discovering the techniques to put my money where my mouth was.

Some people close to me thought I was doing *too much* to my hair. I had a goal, however, and I had prayed on it. I moved towards it with almost military precision and focus. The results speak for themselves.

You do not have to put as much effort into your hair journey as I did (in the first 2 years), but I guarantee you that with even 50 per cent of that effort, you will get results.

What do you have to lose?

If at the end of eight weeks, after putting in the time and effort, your hair is even fractionally better than it was at the beginning, you have already improved on what you had. Now consider if your hair is 1 inch longer *and* thicker than you've ever known, you know you are on the way to greater lengths.

I've already told you what this book is and what it is not. It is time for us to set off on your hair care journey and discover your hair's true health and length potentials.

Before My Hair Journey

April 2006 (Brushing shoulders)   *November 2006* (Just past shoulder length)

My Hair Journey Started at the End of July 2008

September 2008 (2 months into hair journey)   *December* 2008 (5 months into journey)

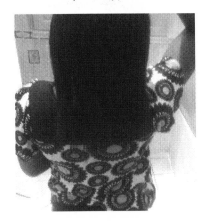

July 2009 (1 year into journey)

December 2009 (1 year and 5 months into journey)

*July 20*10 (2 years into journey)

January 2011 (2.5 years into journey)

August 2012 (4 years on journey)   *August 2012*

Hip length in the back   Waist length in the front

Longest Length in My Life!

Deep Conditioning

Welcome to the first week of your hair journey.

This week I am going to start with something that took my hair to the next level and helped me to *finally* start seeing healthier—and eventually longer—hair. *Deep conditioning*!

Deep conditioning is something I neglected to do for a long time. I used to only deep condition *once or twice a year*—after few relaxer touch-ups had gone by. To put this in context, I had been relaxing my hair since the tender age of 6 and was 24 years old when I embarked on my hair journey! Back then, I relaxed my hair every 8 to 12 weeks.

The conditioning step re-infuses our dry strands of hair with moisture, which can then help them to flow through a week of styling and daily wear and tear. This boost of moisture rejuvenates dry, lacklustre strands, giving it more strength, elasticity, moisture, and softness. It is a really good way of replenishing lost moisture, leaving it less prone to breakage!

By deep conditioning once a week, you too can reap these benefits. You will also notice a huge improvement in the manageability of your hair.

First, *what is deep conditioning?*

Deep conditioning is when you apply a conditioning product to your hair and leave it on for at least 15 minutes to allow your hair to absorb more of its oils and other conditioning ingredients. These ingredients not only smooth the cuticles but also give the inner portions of the strand a boost of moisture.

How?

When heat is applied over the deep conditioner—either externally or by leaving it on under a plastic cap for 30 minutes—your cuticles open up to allow the product to penetrate deeper. Hence the name, deep conditioner!

I want you to keep in mind that any practice you start must be consistently repeated to achieve the results you want. After all, anything that gives you results after only one use can only be classified as 'magic'.

Before I elaborate further on conditioning, however, I want to answer a fundamental question.

Why is Afro hair so dry?

Hair Science

Whether your hair is straight, curly, or kinky in its natural state is determined by the type of follicle it grows from. Hair, being a natural fibre, takes on the shape of its follicle. A cross section of hair looks like an ellipse (see the diagram on the next page). The follicle is located beneath the skin surface and has its own blood supply (from capillaries), bringing it nutrients and oxygen.

Straight hair grows from a circular-shaped follicle, whilst curlier hair types grow from oval-shaped follicles. Furthermore, a flatter (thinner in width) follicle will make hairs that are thinner or flatter. Afro hair tends to grow from follicles that both are oval-shaped and flat (thinner diameter). A good way to understand this is to think of a roll of flat shiny ribbon and a roll of string. The ribbon rolls up very easily, just like the ringlets that grow through a flat, oval follicle, while the string will fall straight when unravelled.

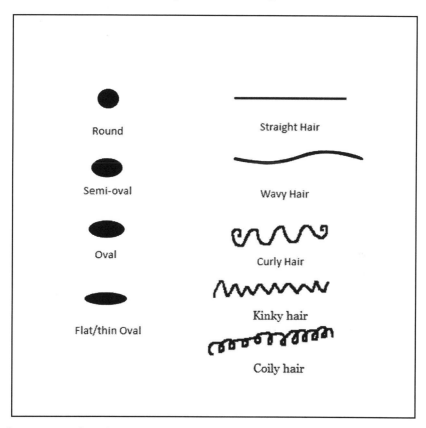

Sebaceous glands are attached to the hair follicles in the skin and scalp. These produce 'sebum', an oily-waxy substance, whose function is to lubricate and protect the hair fibre as well as make the scalp waterproof.

I will now discuss the main hair types found across the races.

Knowing what my hair type and shape was really helped me to grasp how vital moisturised hair was in my haircare practices. There have been a few attempts at classifying the textures. Below is one of the most commonly used systems: the Andre Walker Hair Typing System. In the Appendix, you will find two other hair type classifications.

Andre Walker Hair Typing System: Types 1-4

Type 1: Straight Hair

This hair type has no curl pattern, and this tends to be very sleek and shiny. This is because light can easily reflect off the hair. When straight hair appears dull, it is usually because it is damaged.

Type 2: Wavy Hair

This hair type has a natural loose 'S' curl pattern as it hangs. These can be further classified into 2A (fine), 2B (medium), or 2C (thick and coarse with frizzier). Type 2C is very versatile: style from straight and sleek to tighter curls.

Type 3: Medium Curly Hair

This hair type is often simply described as springy hair. Again, it can be classed as 3A (looser curl), 3B (tighter curl), and 3C hair (tightly curly and kinky). This is often very thick and can be challenging to straighten.

A blow-dry followed by a flat iron will give a smoother finish.

Type 4: Kinky, Coily Hair

Type 4 hairs are tightly coiled, much coarser, and look thicker than other hair types. However, it is actually quite fine with thin strands. It is further divided into types 4A ('S' pattern), 4B (wiry with zigzag kinky pattern), and 4C hair (tiny coils). This hair type has fewer protective cuticle layers and can easily break when combed or brushed.

Type 4 is the most adaptable hair type, often holding styles without the need for styling products. Types 3 and 4 hairs can absorb a lot of water when they are wet. This also causes them to shrink up to 40 per cent of their stretched length. They also do not tend to look shiny as they don't reflect light as the straighter hair types.

Do note that most black women have more than one curl pattern or type on their head. This brings us back to our original question.

Why is Afro hair dry?

The sebum produced by the follicle finds it harder to make its way down curly hair, which can be likened to the bends of a spring than straighter hair types. As it cannot jump across these springs, the hair loses some of its moisture when exposed to the elements: sun, wind, and clothing. This dryness can lead to brittle hair.

Furthermore, if your hair is chemically processed—relaxed, colour-treated, or texturised—it is even more prone to dryness as the cuticles are already damaged. These are all factors that mean Afro-textured hair needs some extra moisture regularly.

Enough facts, back to deep conditioning!

How to Deep Condition Your Hair

Tools

You only need a few tools.

These include: sectioning clips, shower cap, spray bottle, and a conditioner (of your choice).

1. You can start with damp or dry hair. If dry, spritz with water.
2. Part hair into 4 to 8 sections (according to hair length) and secure with sectioning clips. You can also twist or braid each section to secure it.
3. Apply conditioner to the ends of the hair on one section (lower 1/3rd of the hair).
4. Apply more conditioner to the rest of the hair (root and body of hair) and secure this section out of the way with a clip.
5. Repeat steps 2-4 throughout head.
6. Cover hair with shower cap or plastic bag.

7. Leave on for 15-30 minutes.
8. Remove clips and rinse hair thoroughly with warm water and pat dry with a soft towel or dry T-shirt.

Optional Steps

- Warm up a damp towel (microwave for 20-30seconds) and wrap around your head over the shower cap.
- Sit under a steaming cap for 30 minutes.
- Leave conditioner on your hair for 1 hour (cover shower cap with a beanie hat) while you do some household chores.

How Does It Work?

A deep conditioner has ingredients in it that can penetrate the hair shaft to replace moisture and add some fatty acids or protein where needed. By leaving on for 15-30 minutes, you allow your hair cuticle to open up and absorb more conditioner. With some heat, this opening occurs quicker. When left on hair for an hour without heat, your body temperature heats up the hair—with the plastic bag keeping the warmth from the scalp—and you get the benefit of a steam treatment.

Your hair will feel smoother and softer once it has absorbed the moisture from the conditioner.

This will make styling it for the week so much easier. Furthermore, your strands are less dry, brittle, and prone to breaking in one step!

Now it's time to tackle the first hair myth that is a major stumbling block for most black women.

Hair Myth #1: 'Black Hair Cannot Grow Long!'

I have found this fallacy has grown in popularity because of the numerous bad haircare practices in the black community. Our hair types cannot be handled like the others; neither can it be neglected without obvious effect.

When nurtured properly—with simple steps—it will thrive and grow. My hair is proof enough for me, but I initially had to take proof from other heads of hair.

You have probably noticed that a woman who maintains straight hair with a relaxer goes for touch-ups every 8 weeks. This is because there is 'new growth' at the roots, which do not match the relaxed hair strands below.

If this new growth was allowed to grow out for six months, you would have three inches of textured roots—with an average growth rate. When straightened, the added length will now be visible. This only occurs if you have consistently moisturised the already-relaxed length and kept it strong during the grow-out period. I noticed this when I waited for three months between relaxers.

The main message here is not to focus solely on the growth but to *pay attention to the ends* of your strands. When properly handled, you retain them. With intact ends and new growth, you will see longer hair.

Ends care + New growth = Length retention.

Here are a few of the deep conditioners I have tried with good results. Below them are a few recipes for homemade deep conditioning treatments. I recommend any of these highly.

Suggested Deep Conditioners

- Le Kair Cholesterol
- Giovanni Smooth as Silk Conditioner
- Keracare Humecto
- Herbal Essences Hello Hydration Conditioner and 3 tablespoons of extra virgin olive oil (add one tablespoon to each palm-full of conditioner).

- Crème of Nature Nourishing Conditioner
- Elasta QP DPR-11
- Pantene Relaxed and Natural Mask
- Aubrey Organics Honeysuckle Rose Conditioner

Deep-conditioning Recipes

1. **Avocado and Coconut Treat**
   Ingredients: 1 peeled and mashed avocado and 1 cup coconut milk.
   Directions: Combine mashed avocado with some coconut milk in a small bowl (a hand blender will make it smoother). Warm up in microwave for around 30 to 45 seconds. Stir well and test temperature against the back of your hand before use. Massage mixture into hair. Cover with shower cap for 15-30 minutes. Shampoo and rinse out.

2. **Honey Deep Conditioner**
   Ingredients: 3-4 tablespoons of honey and extra virgin olive oil.
   Directions: Place jar of honey in a cup of hot water before mixing (makes it runnier). Start with damp hair. Mix in palm of hands and apply to section of hair. Mix more and apply!

3. **Coconut Honey Deep Conditioner**
   Ingredients: 4 tablespoons of coconut oil and 2 tablespoons of natural honey.
   Directions: Place coconut oil and honey in a small plastic bag and place the bag in a cup of hot water (not boiling) for 1 minute to warm. Apply to hair, cover hair with a shower cap, and warm with a towel for 20 minutes. Wash hair and then gently dry and style as usual.

Week One Learning Points

- Deep conditioning is a way to revitalise and moisturise dry strands.
- There are various hair types and textures, and they require different handling techniques.

- Afro-textured hair tends to dryness owing to poorer lubrication by sebum from the scalp.
- Afro-textured hair will benefit from regular deep conditioning.
- Poor hair-handling practices have led to poor retention of the hair ends through breakage.
- Black hair can grow long.

Action Plan for Week One

- Take a picture of your hair at the start of this journey. I recommend:

    — One picture with your hair in a straightened state, from the back, showing the length
    — A second picture from the front, showing the length.

- Buy or mix a deep-conditioning treatment and follow the steps above.
- Enjoy the feel of your freshly conditioned hair!
- Pick a day of the week to designate as your deep-conditioning day (Sundays are good). Commit to deep condition every week of your hair journey.

WEEK TWO:

Clean Scalp and Hair

We will start this week with a myth that I find a bit appalling but, surprisingly, is held on to with conviction by many ladies.

Hair Myth #2: 'Washing Your Hair Too Often Won't Let It Grow!'

A clean scalp is the perfect environment for hair to grow at its best. Many are told not to wash their hair too much because 'our hair gets too dry that way'. Countless others have been told for years that 'dirt' and 'grease' makes your hair grow. No, that just gives you smelly, product-laden hair!

Washing your hair at least weekly gives you a great foundation for your haircare routine. When you apply moisturising and nourishing products to *clean* hair, you will get better results! For instance, you would not be able to get smooth hair with a certain product if it couldn't get past the dirt on your hair.

Furthermore, when your scalp is clean, your hair can grow at its optimum rate.

How to Wash Your Hair

Sounds like teaching you to walk, right? However, a lot of poor practices whilst washing your hair will continue to sabotage your hair growth (length retention) efforts.

I will show you how to effectively clean your hair and scalp without drying out your tresses.

1. Part hair into 4-8 sections and secure with clips or in twists or braids.
2. Wet hair with warm water (shower is best), then shut off the water source.
3. Apply cleanser to your scalp, move through all sections.
4. Gently massage into scalp using pads of fingers (never use nails)!
5. Step back under the shower stream.
6. Smooth the cleanser down your hair (never upwards).
7. Undo one section of hair at a time and rinse.
8. Squeeze excess water from each section, apply deep conditioner and re-twist or re-braid.

Choosing Your Cleanser

Shampoo is not the only way to wash your hair! I'm sorry if I've shocked you, but it really isn't.

Shampoo was initially formulated for the Caucasian hair types to remove sebum and product build-up. I know that the average black woman has her share of products that she uses on a semi-regular basis. Unfortunately, a lot of the products that promise to tame frizz and smooth our hair are laden with mineral oil and silicones. These definitely need to be cleansed from the hair.

Sulphates are a main ingredient in soaps, detergents, and, you guessed it, shampoos. They are very strong cleansers. After only one rinse, black hair usually feels dry and stripped to touch—with all the natural oils removed from around the cuticle. Furthermore, shampoos are usually more alkaline than our hair strands prefer (optimum pH 4.5-5.5). This makes the cuticles stand up and causes friction when strands rub against each other, thereby making the hair more prone to breaking.

As I said, shampoos are not all there is!

You can use sulphate-free cleansers to clean your hair. Another option is using hair rinses such as apple cider vinegar or baking soda. A tablespoon of either in a cup of water will effectively remove dirt. You can also use conditioner to wash your hair. It has enough surfactant to remove dirt in your hair. However, you need to massage the scalp well to get it clean with conditioner.

Finally, you can use clay hair masks like bentonite clay or rhassoul clay. See Appendix for more details on clay masks and their benefits.

If you do decide to use shampoo as your cleanser, here are some ways to minimise its ill effects:

- Try diluting a capful of shampoo in a cup of water and use it to cleanse your hair. This also works well for protective styles like box braids—you apply this to the roots, massage gently, and rinse.
- Choose a *moisturising* shampoo, formulated for dry hair. These are usually less stripping.
- If using a *clarifying* shampoo to remove a lot of product build-up, one rinse is all that you need. Another name is a *'volumising'* shampoo.
- A *neutralising* shampoo—aimed for use after a relaxer touch-up—is pH balanced (try Organic Root Stimulator Creamy Aloe Shampoo).
- Always condition your hair afterwards to smooth the cuticle.

Learning Points for Week Two

- A clean scalp is a good background for healthy hair growth.
- Shampoos can often be too harsh for the Afro hair textures; there are alternatives.
- Always apply your cleanser to the roots and scalp before rinsing to work the product down the hair.
- If you use a lot of products regularly, do clarify to remove their build-up (once a month is plenty).

- *Always follow with conditioner* (rinse out or deep condition).

Action Plan for Week Two

- Cleanse your hair with your chosen cleanser before deep conditioning.

  — If you are going to use shampoo, try diluting it first.
  — If you are using a new cleanser, keep using it every week if it cleans your hair without stripping it.

- Start a hair journal (Use the template below as a guide.) 'Write the vision and make it plain on tablets, that he may run who reads it.' (Habakkuk 2: 2)

  — Write down the start date of your hair journey: deep condition day 1.
  — Add your short-term hair goals for the 1-2 months: thicker hair, shiny hair, or easier to style.
  — Add your long-term hair goals: for example, how long you would like your hair to grow or being able to put your hair in a bun.

Your First Hair Journal

I find that having a monthly plan is the best way to start off your journey.

You can then make changes to parts of your new routine on a monthly basis. The basic outline remains the same from month to month, but you may decide to add in a new product or technique for a few weeks.

Your hair journal only needs to be an A5 notepad that you can carry around with you.

Month:

Hair Goals (Write on the First Page)

- Short-term
- Long-term

Weekly Routine (Second Page)

- Daily moisture and sealing: how often?
- Weekly wash and deep condition
- Any co-washing: how often?

Chosen Protective Style(s) (Next Page)

New Techniques (Beneath Chosen Protective Styles)

- How often? What will it achieve?

Document on another page what your current products are. For example:

Technique	Product	Frequency
Moisturising shampoo and cleanser	E.g. ORS Creamy Aloe	E.g. Once a week
Moisturising rinse-out conditioner and co-wash		
Moisturising deep conditioner		
Protein treatment		
Leave-in conditioner		
Moisturiser		
Sealing oil		
Clarifying cleanser (remove build-up)		

WEEK THREE:

Daily Moisture Routine

Welcome to week three of your hair journey. By now, you are probably noticing your properly conditioned hair feels better than the previously stripped dry hair post-shampoo. I'm going to introduce the next essential part of your journey: *developing a daily moisture routine.*

How important *is* a five-minute daily routine in caring for your hair?

To me, it's the difference between having a map in the car and actually using it!

Imagine you have decided to start saving money at the start of a new year. You put aside one penny (1p) every day in a jar. At the end of the year, you have three hundred and sixty-five pence (365 p) or £3.65. You opt to buy a new pair of earrings with this—on sale, of course!

Now imagine you put aside one pound (£1) each day instead of a penny. At the end of the year, you have three hundred and sixty-five pounds, £365, instead of three pounds and sixty-five pence (£3.65). What you could do with that amount: go on holiday, buy a new piece of furniture, or update your wardrobe!

You will notice the same degree of improvement between a weekly and daily moisture routine.

The routine needs only five (5) minutes a day? Well, it's true! In some hairstyles, my routine takes even less time.

Why should I moisturise my hair daily?

Research suggests that Afro hair follicles seem to produce the most sebum of all the hair types. As I mentioned before in the deep-conditioning week, these natural oils cannot easily make their way down the hair strands.

You have probably also noticed that when you put a moisturising product in your hair, it tends to feel dry within a few hours of leaving the house. This is because the elements—the sun, wind, and your clothing—can 'pull' moisture from your hair.

For this reason, Afro-textured hair benefits from applying some oil on top of the moisturiser to 'seal in' the moisture. The term 'seal' really just speaks of its ability to delay the drying out process.

Hair that is properly moisturised will be infinitely easier to manage and will be less prone to breaking—the major cause for not realising our hair length goals.

Hair Science

On average, hair grows at approximately half an inch a month. Your hair may grow slightly faster (0.75 in) or slower (0.25 in) than this due to genetic, nutritional, and environmental factors. Therefore, every 2 months (8 weeks) you should be seeing an inch of growth.

For instance, you may have noted 'fast growers' in your family or that your hair goes through a growth spurt in summer months. However, if you are not getting a balanced diet—with all your essential vitamins and minerals—you may not have yet experienced your optimal growth rate.

Final fact for this week:

The ends of your hair are the oldest parts of the hair strand.

By the time it reaches your shoulders, it has seen 1 to 2 years of growth! If you had a *silk scarf* you wore *daily* and washed *weekly,* you would expect it to lose its original shape and colour in two years!

Yet by moisturising your hair daily, you reinforce the strands with elasticity to weather the daily wear and tear.

Hair Myth #3: 'A Growth Aid—That's All I Need to Get Long Hair'

A *'growth aid'* is the term used to describe products that are purported to speed up the rate of one's hair growth. The rationale behind this is that if used for a short while, you will reap amazing results in hair length.

My usual response to such promises is:

Anything that sounds too good to be true usually IS.

There are many products marketed for hair growth: either for oral consumption or for topical application (to the scalp). Claims about ingredients such as sulphur, antifungals, and certain proteins are that they will speed up one's hair growth. The results are usually not as dramatic as advertised. You will not get mid-back length hair overnight!

Some people find that they achieve some growth (an inch or two over a couple of months) with these products, but the main concern is that few people actually wonder why they are getting these results.

Sulphur, for instance, is an important building block in hair, with 35 per cent of its amino acids having sulphur in them. If one's diet is lacking in sulphur, oral sulphur supplementation, like MSM

(*Methylsulphonylmethane*), or applying it directly to the scalp will positively affect the hair strand: by helping the hair follicle to form new healthy hair cells. Keratin in the hair strands are linked by strong *disulphide* (*sulphur*) bonds.

Simple multivitamins and mineral tablets will also affect the rate of one's hair growth if you *were* deficient in them. If you are not deficient in any of these, your growth rate will not change.

Other topical 'growth aids' are usually found not to have much of an effect if you remove *one key factor*: frequent washing and conditioning of the hair. By rinsing or washing your hair three times a week after applying a product to your scalp its moisture content increases. The extra length retention you notice is down to the washing and conditioning, not necessarily the product.

Whether your hair is growing at 0.5 inches a month or not (faster or slower), if your ends are still breaking, you remain at square one. Growth aids do not equal better length retention. A good haircare regime does.

How to Moisturise and Seal Your Hair

Your daily moisture regimen will change depending on how you choose to wear your hair.

I will highlight three main routines, which you can tweak to suit your particular hair-styling preference, be it relaxed or natural. I know ladies with natural hair sometimes opt for straight styles and relaxed ladies may opt for textured styles so I've taken this into account for each routine.

The main difference between these routines is the kind of the moisturiser you are applying (spray or lotion or cream). You may also find that you want to swap these routines in certain protective styles. Feel free to experiment between these three!

Tools You Will Need

- Sectioning clips
- Moisturising lotion or cream
- Natural oil or butter mix
- Spray bottle
- Water (for your moisturising spray mixes)

Routine 1: For Relaxed or Straightened Styles

1. Divide your hair into 2-4 sections.
2. Apply a quarter-size (2 penny coin) of your chosen moisturising lotion to the palm of your hand.
3. Rub the palms together to spread it out.
4. Apply initially to the ends of one section, then closer to the root.
5. Smooth lotion from the roots down your hair.
6. Use a clip to hold that section apart and repeat steps 2-5 on other sections.
7. Now apply a dime-size of oil to your palm and rub both palms together.
8. Apply it to the first section's ends, then roots and smooth down.
9. Repeat on all sections. Your hair is now moisturised!

Routine 2: For Natural Hair or Textured Styles (Braid-outs and Twist-outs)

1. Divide hair into 2-4 sections.
2. Using a spray bottle, make your moisturising mix (see next section).
3. Holding spray bottle at arm's length, lightly spritz one section once or twice.
4. Apply a chosen hair butter or oil to the ends and then the roots of the hair.
5. Braid or twist that section loosely.
6. Repeat steps 3-5 on the remaining sections.

Routine 3: For Protective Styles (Braids or Twists or Weaves)

1. Divide the hair into 4 sections.
2. Make your moisturising mix in a spray bottle.
3. Spray this mix on to a section of your hair.
4. If you are wearing a weave, lift the hair to expose the braids beneath the weft and spray lightly.
5. You do not need to apply oils to your hair in extensions as this will only cause dust and dirt to gather.
6. You can apply some oil to the edges of your hair (where your hair is exposed).

You now have the basic steps for moisturising and sealing your hair every day.

You may repeat these steps once or twice a day (in the mornings and evenings). I have heard a few ladies say they moisturise their hair three times a day, but I feel that borders on the excessive side. I know how daunting it can be to pick products in the average beauty supply store so I will make a few suggestions of affordable moisturisers below.

What happens to my daily routine on wash days?

It's simple really! I moisturise and seal in the morning as usual. When I wash my hair later in the day, I use a leave-in conditioner instead of my moisturiser after deep conditioning. I will discuss leave-in conditioners in the heat-free styling week.

What about at night-time?

I know a lot of haircare routines get *frustrated* by the night-time considerations.

Keep it simple!

Your hair will keep in the moisture you apply before bed if you protect your hair ends at night. How? Invest a couple of pounds in a satin scarf or bonnet! These can be found in most beauty supply stores in a variety of colours. Simply, apply a scarf over your hair before bedtime and wake up with smooth hair.

Sleeping for 6-8 hours on a cotton pillowcase *will* dry out our already vulnerable hair. Satin or silk does not pull the moisture from our strands and keeps the hair smoothly in place. If your scarf falls off midway through the night, cover it with a bonnet. It will stay put! (Tried and tested.)

If the thought of sleeping with a scarf or bonnet goes against all your ideas of 'cute', then buy a satin pillowcase instead. You get the same effect without the bonnet look! (See, I've got your back!) Satin pillowcases are now sold at many beauty supply stores, but you can also get them online.

Suggested Moisturisers

- Herbal Essences Long Term Relationship.
- S Curl Moisturizing Lotion: glycerine-rich (beware with humidity).
- Wave Nouveau Moisturizing Lotion: glycerine-rich (again, be wary of humidity).
- Organic Root Stimulator: Oil Moisturising Lotion.
- *Moisturising mixes:* choose from

  — Water alone.
  — The 'Juice': in a spray bottle, mix 200 ml water and 30 ml of aloe vera juice. Store in fridge between uses and use up in one week. You can also add 1-2 tablespoons of glycerine.
  — Water and glycerine (be wary in humid climates)—1-2 tablespoons in 100 ml of water.
  — Water and a moisturising lotion—dilute a capful in 200 ml of water and use a spray bottle to dispense.

Suggested Oils and Butters

- *Extra Virgin Olive (Olea europaea) Oil:* known for its skin moisturising benefits, giving smoothness and softness to dry skin and hair.

- *Extra Virgin Coconut (Cocos nuciferas) Oil:* it has been found to reduce protein loss from hair when used for pre—and post-shampoo hair grooming (http://journal.scconline.org/pdf/cc2003/cc054n02/p00175-p00192.pdf). As a triglyceride of lauric acid, its high affinity for protein and its low molecular weight allows it to penetrate the hair shaft (http://www.ncbi.nlm.nih.gov/pubmed/12715094). It has high-saturated fat content allowing it to last up to 2 years.

- *Jojoba (Simmondsia chenensis) Oil:* it is actually a *liquid wax* and is quite shelf-stable as it has no triglycerides in it. As it is very similar to sebum, it can 'fool' the skin into thinking it has produced this oil and thereby balance oil production—hence, it is non-comedogenic (http://www.acne.org/jojoba-oil.php).

- *Sunflower (*Helianthus annuus*) Oil:* it is high in Vitamin E and low in saturated fat. It has been shown to help retain moisture in the skin and creates a protective barrier against infections (http://www.medscape.org/viewarticle/501077). It is also a natural source of ceramides—protective fatty acids on hair.

- *Grapeseed (Vitis vinifera) Oil:* high in fatty acids and a source of Vitamin E leaves a glossy layer on skin and hair when applied lightly.

- *Castor (Ricinus communis) Oil:* owing to its low molecular weight, it is able to penetrate deep into the skin. Many women have used castor oil on their roots and reported thickening of their hair and hair growth (http://www.castoroilhome.com/castor-oil-hair-growth-treatment).

- *Avocado (Persea Americana) Oil:* it is rich in monounsaturated fats and Vitamins A, D, and E. Often used in cosmetics for its moisturising properties but is also a rich source of protein and lecithin (http://en.wikipedia.org/wiki/Avocado_oil).

- *Shea Butter (Butyrospermum parkii):* this thick butter which melts at body temperature is derived from the nut of the Karite tree. It has a high lipid profile with Vitamin A and oleic acid (omega-9 fatty acid). Some compounds within it confer UVB protection ~ SPF 6-15. It is quite moisturising, emollient, and softening for skin and hair.

Learning Points for Week Three

- A daily moisturiser will really boost the manageability of your hair.
- Sealing in moisture with oil will keep your hair moisturised for longer.
- Water is a simple but great moisturiser.
- Your night-time routine will prevent your hair from drying out overnight.

Action Plan for Week Three

- Choose your moisturiser or mix.
- Invest in a satin scarf, bonnet, or pillowcase. The choice is yours!
- I also recommend getting a spray bottle—they always come in handy.
- Start moisturising your hair this week: I suggest tomorrow at the latest.
- Only make enough of your moisture spray-mix to last a week. If aloe vera juice is in it, store in the fridge between uses. Pour away after a week has passed and make a fresh batch.

WEEK FOUR:

Protein Treatments

You are now halfway through this jump-start to your hair journey. This week, we are going to focus on something that has been known to make or break (excuse the pun) the hair journey:

Understanding the importance of protein!

The most common setback for many women with Afro-textured hair, whether rocking it in its natural state, relaxed, or texturised, is 'breakage'!

'Breakage' is a term—coined on haircare forums and boards—used to describe seeing lots of small broken off pieces of hair on the floor or in a detangling tool with minimal manipulation. This is disheartening for even the most diehard haircare fan! When hair is breaking, the health of the strand is usually lacking. I say 'usually' because nutritional factors as well as stress can sometimes lead to breakage in otherwise healthy hair!

Simply put, your hair will break wherever there are points of weakness within the strand.

After years of noticing tiny hairs on my shoulders and on the bathroom floor, I was done with it! You should be too!

There are three main causes of breakage:

1. *Dry hair*: loses its elasticity (stretching ability) for those styling sessions.
2. *Weak hair*: loses its strength to withstand even minor stresses.
3. *Poor hair-handling practices*: even very healthy hair cannot withstand some of our hair 'abuse'.

Dry hair has been tackled in the first three weeks. The third will be discussed in weeks five and six. I will tackle weak hair with you now so your hair will never be described that way again.

I grew out my relaxed hair over 2 years and 8 months and I kept my relaxed ends intact! Most people—quite a few being hair care professionals—would tell you that this feat was impossible. Now you and I both know it is *not (see hip length pictures at the beginning of the book)*!

Now, I don't want you to think that you will never see hairs in your comb again!

Hair Science

Our hair follicles go through a growth cycle that involves a growing phase (*anagen*), a resting phase (*catagen*), and a shedding phase (*telogen*). Between the resting and shedding phase, the base of the shrunken follicle moves upwards in the skin until it released from the scalp. The hair cycle can last anything from 3 to 6 years! Inevitably, at any point in time, there will be some follicles going through the shedding phase (about 5-10 per cent). Hence, you *will* see these hairs in your comb.

So what is the difference between shedding hair and breakage?

On average, we shed about 50-100 strands of hair a day. Those numbers sound scary until you remember that we have around 100,000 strands of hair on our heads (some people have a lot more than this!). At any one point in time, 80-90 per cent of our hairs are in the growing phase. However, each hair can become broken anywhere along its length at any time during the hair growth cycle.

A shed hair (*exogen*) can be distinguished from a broken hair in a number of ways:

1. Shed hairs have a white bulb from the root on one end of the hair.
2. Shed hairs are usually longer than the broken hairs (which tend to break off lower down the strand).
3. Broken hairs usually have visible splits in them—split ends.

Let's talk about weak hair strands. I'll give you a quick low-down on hair's natural structure.

The Hair Strand

Hair is mainly made up of dead cells (keratinocytes), protein (*Keratin*), and pigment. These protein molecules are arranged in an intricate way to give it both an elasticity (ability to stretch) and plasticity (ability to withstand pulling forces without breaking). Of course, hair is a natural fibre so it has a limit to both of these abilities. Even healthy hair will break at each limit, but that would take an unnatural amount of pulling force on the strands.

The outermost layer of the hair strand is the *cuticle,* and this cell layer is arranged like shingles on a roof (facing away from the scalp). There are several layers of cells forming the cuticle. It has a smooth surface that helps to minimise friction between the hair strands and gives the hair its sheen—or shine in straighter hair types. The cuticle keeps the moisture within the hair shaft. This moisture provides a lot of its elastic properties.

The intermediate layer is called the *cortex*. This gives the hair most of its thickness, length, and strength (due to the keratin in it) as well as its colour (from pigment within). The innermost layer of the hair shaft is the *medulla,* though this is often not present in fine or thin hair strands. Interestingly, the medulla contributes the least to the mechanical and chemical properties of the hair.

Below is a diagrammatic representation of the hair strand in cross section.

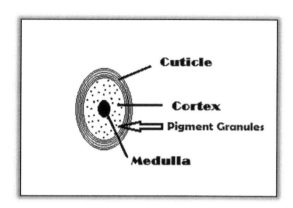

An intact cuticle keeps the central portion of the hair protected from environmental damage.

The cuticle is usually the initial site of damage when applying chemical processes such as colour or relaxers. When hair is subjected to heat or regular poor handling, the bonds within the strands become weakened, leaving it prone to breaking.

At the ends of the hair, when the cuticle is worn down, the hair shaft can literally split into two. The split area is now a point of weakness where the hair can easily break off with minor manipulation. These split ends can, unfortunately, be a bane of hair length goals. If not taken care of promptly, the split can widen upwards, making more of the hair strand weak!

This brings us to the hair myth of the week.

Hair Myth #4: 'Cutting Your Hair Will Make It Grow (Faster)!'

This is pure fallacy! The origin of this myth has such a tiny speck of truth that it has been happily propagated across the seas. In fact, many haircare professionals will tell you this without a qualm.

This myth arose because *split ends can only be managed one way—by trimming them*! They cannot be mended, glued back together (as some products claim), or be nursed back to health.

Below is a chart showing different kinds of splitting ends:

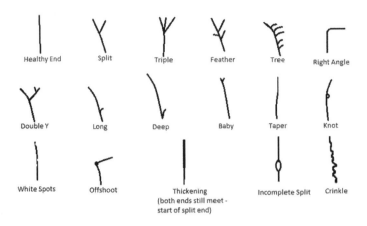

However, I must stress the fact that trims differ from a haircut! Most split ends *can be sorted out by trimming a quarter to half an inch (¼ - ½ inch)* off the offending pieces of hair. A haircut, on the other hand, removes inches of hair at a time!

The second argument against this myth is that hair growth occurs at the scalp! *Only the scalp!* Once hair is past the scalp, it is on its own! Hair is a dead fibre that we preserve for aesthetic purposes. Like silk, it requires delicate care for it to thrive and look good. Cutting the ends will not speed its descent down from the scalp.

The bottom line is that *split ends are not your friends.*

Scissors, when lightly applied, will rid you of them. Those scissors should never rid you of length unless you want a new look!

Let's focus on protein for now. Proteins are the major building blocks of hair. The breaking of the bonds in the hair leads to protein loss. Thus, incorporating a protein treatment once in a while will make a noticeable difference.

Protein Treatments

Protein treatments are very much like conditioners, but they focus on putting some protein into the hair shaft instead of moisture. These treatments often have amino acids or hydrolysed (water-soluble) versions of the proteins they are infusing to make the process of absorption into the hair shaft easier. Some conditioners also have added proteins in them.

A protein treatment is only needed once a month and you apply it in much the same way as a deep conditioner. The main difference is that you must apply the protein treatment before you shampoo or wash your hair. Why? Protein tends to make the hair move towards the harder side of its spectrum between elasticity and plasticity. After the treatment, you need to remove the excess protein on the hair shaft (that was not absorbed) and deep condition to reinfuse moisture (elasticity).

You may hear or see the above effect on hair described regularly among hair care circles as *the moisture—protein balance.*

In weeks 1 and 3, I have focussed on getting your hair's moisture levels up because this is usually the first culprit for daily breakage. The second is weak hair (protein loss).

If your hair has had any chemical treatments recently, the protein bonds broken during these processes require a regular protein treatment schedule. I recommend doing one within a week of each chemical treatment—for example, one week after a relaxer touch-up.

How to Apply a Protein Treatment

1. Start with damp hair—step under shower for 1 minute and squeeze out the excess water.
2. Section hair with your hands into 4 sections.
3. Apply a half palm-sized amount of your treatment to the ends and then the roots of one section.
4. Secure with a hair clip or in twists or braids.

5. Repeat steps 3 and 4 in the remaining sections.
6. Leave treatment on for 15 to 30 minutes under a plastic cap.
7. You can sit under a hood dryer, steamer cap, or put a warm damp towel over the plastic cap.
8. Rinse well and follow with a cleanser and deep-conditioning session.

Suggested Protein Treatments

(I have personally tried all of these in my time!)

- Any product that have the words: 'Strengthening' or 'Reconstructor' in the name.
- Aphogee Keratin 2 minute Reconstructor.
- Motions CPR Treatment (Critical Protection and Repair).
- ORS (Organic Root Stimulator) Replenishing Pak or Replenishing Conditioner (in a bottle).
- 'Organics' (African Pride) Hair Mayonnaise.
- ORS Hair Mayonnaise.
- Original Mane 'n' Tail Conditioner.
- Aubrey Organics Glycogen Protein Balancing (GPB) Conditioner.

Recipes: Protein Treatments at Home

1. *Just add eggs:* add one egg (or two if hair is longer than armpit length) to your regular deep conditioner. Mix it up in a bowl, apply, and leave on for 15-30 minutes *without heat* under *a plastic cap*. Rinse and then cleanse and deep condition.
2. *Coconut oil wonder:* simply melt 3-5 tablespoons of coconut oil in a small bowl and apply to damp hair, focussing on the ends. Cover with a plastic cap for 20-30 minutes, preferably with heat. Rinse, cleanse, and deep condition.
3. *Avocado punch:* you will need a small jar of mayonnaise and half an avocado. Mash the avocado and mix it with mayonnaise in a medium-sized bowl (alternatively, use a hand blender or food processor) until it's a consistent green

colour. Smooth into hair and cover with a shower cap or plastic wrap for 20-30 minutes (with or without heat). Freeze any extra mix and use within 1-2 weeks.

Learning Points from Week 4

- Hair of Afro-Caribbean origin benefits from monthly protein treatments to strengthen it.
- Spilt ends can only be trimmed off—protein only helps prevent them from forming.
- Shedding is natural, but breakage is not!
- Always follow a protein treat with a cleanser and moisturising deep condition.
- When choosing your protein treatment, I recommend you to buy the small sample packs first.

Action Plan for Week 4

- Pick your protein treatment: surprising what's in your kitchen or local beauty supply store!
- Follow the steps above and do your first protein treatment of this journey.
- Write in your hair journal how your hair feels after you have cleansed and conditioned.

  Note down the name (or recipe) of your protein treatment: you will be repeating it in week 8!

WEEK FIVE:

Heat-free Styling

Week five is exciting as it will show you how to make your hair styling less stressful—both for you and your hair. I will initially focus on *reducing the use of heat for styling purposes*. Then it's time to introduce new ways to achieve the same look with little or no heat.

Heat styling is something that has set back many a woman on her journey to healthier, longer tresses. The problem is that most women don't know the dangers of heat to their hair. Neither are they aware of where to draw the line between heat styling and heat 'abuse'.

Repeated misuse of heated tools is easy to see on a person with naturally curly or kinky hair. Their hair simply loses its ability to return to its usual curl or kink pattern. This hair will dry out easier and also tends to be more prone to breakage with the same amount of styling. Moisture in our strands keeps them soft and manageable—heated appliances will rob our hair of this.

Why can heat be so detrimental to healthy hair?

Hair Science

The hair strand (hair shaft) is a structure which grows from root to tip. It is composed of three concentric cell layers: the cuticle, the cortex, and the medulla. The proteins in hair are held in their characteristic shapes by various bonds between the amino acids—the building blocks of every protein chain. There are three bonds which give the hair strands its strength and elasticity: hydrogen bonds, salt bonds, and disulphide bonds. Hydrogen and salt bonds are temporary weak bonds, but they make up the majority of the bonds in each strand.

Hydrogen bonds can be broken by heat or water but will readily reform or reshape with drying and cooling the hair. This is why hair can be 'set' using rollers and will take on that curl pattern from these when dry. It also explains how blow-drying works.

Salt bonds are those which can be broken by changes in pH—how acidic or alkaline the medium on the hair is. The cuticle (outer layer of the hair) rises and lowers with changes in pH. These bonds will reform once you normalise the pH of the hair. Note: hair prefers an acidic pH of around 4.0-5.5, while water is 7, and relaxer is around 12!

Finally, *disulphide bonds* are the strongest bonds in the hair strand. They hold the amino acids together within the chains (polypeptides) that form the protein. Unfortunately, *once these bonds are broken, they cannot be reformed*! Are you wondering what could affect these bonds? Relaxers, texturizers, and strong colour treatments—especially going from black or brown to blonde!

Though heat will temporarily break the hydrogen bonds in hair, when over-used, the disulphide bonds in hair can also be affected. Do note that they won't necessarily be affected to the same degree as with chemical processes. However, repeatedly applying heat directly to the hair strands will create more and more bond breaks, leading to 'heat damage'—permanent changes to the hair's structure that weaken it.

Heat Damage and Hair-styling Tools

Heat damage makes the hair strands more liable to drying out, splitting, and breaking.

The main culprits when discussing heated hair-styling tools that are often over-used include blow-dryers, flat irons, and curling irons or tongs.

Now, not *all* heat is bad! Safer forms of heat are available.

The tools listed above focus the heat directly on the hair shaft. These are termed 'direct heat' tools. 'Indirect heat' tools, such as hooded dryers and steam-powered curlers, work by spreading the heat evenly around the entire head.

Using 'direct' forms of heat does not spell the end of the road for your hair though! It is the misuse and over-use of this form of heat that can lead down that slippery slope of heat damage. Add the cumulative effect of heat and chemical processes, and you are in Breakage Ville (or Split-end City, your choice)!

Minimising Heat Damage

There are ways to safely use direct heat. The main way is to reserve heat styling for special occasions only. There will be occasions where you need your hair to be fully styled quickly. Please remember that this should not be the case *every* day!

Always start by correctly towel drying your hair. To do this, you must gently wrap the hair in the towel (or t-shirt) whilst it hangs downwards and gently squeeze it until it is damp. Never rub it upwards or massage it in the towel—undue friction will lead to more tangles. Then follow by gently detangling with a wide-tooth comb or detangling brush (see week 6 for detangling how to).

Always use a 'leave-in conditioner' before styling your hair. The leave-in conditioner will smoothe your hair and last until your next hair-wash day. It will also help your hair to dry without as many flyaways. A protein-based 'leave-in' will strengthen your hair, whilst a moisturising 'leave-in' will boost the softness of your hair. You should never underestimate the benefits of a good leave-in conditioner.

Next, *always use a 'heat protectant'*. These products have ingredients—usually silicones—which absorb some of the damaging effects of the heated tool whilst also allowing your style to last longer by smoothing the cuticle.

Finally, choose *the correct hair tools* and use them in *the correct way*.

Choosing your Heat Styling Tools

Blow-Dryers

In his book, *The Hair Bible*, Philip Kingsley—often referred to as the 'hair doctor'—recommends the following criteria for choosing your next handheld hair dryer:

- 'It should have separate controls for temperature and speed.'
- You don't need anything stronger than 1,200 watts.
- 'Special diffuser attachments . . . spread the heat over a wider area.'

For using a blow-dryer on Afro-textured hair, I recommend:

- Work in sections and use the lowest heat setting at the highest speed.
- Hold the dryer at half-arm's length (approximately 6 inches) from your hair—arm held at a right angle.
- If you can, only dry your hair from wet to damp or to around 90 per cent dryness to prevent excess moisture loss.
- If you are drying curly or coily hair, try a diffuser. It will be faster to dry but helps to clump the curls.
- Don't focus the heat on your ends. That will dry them out and cause breakage.

Flat or Curling Irons

Flat irons are used to straighten the hair by removing some moisture from the hair whilst pulling the strand straight. In order for them to do this, they must be heated to the correct heat. Needless to say, in the wrong hands, a lot of damage can be done to the hair strands. Curling irons use the same principle to reshape the hair. For straightening the hair, it is recommended that hair is relatively dry. After all, it will need some intrinsic moisture to prevent it from becoming hard with the heat applied.

Philip Kingsley recommends *'steam-producing'* irons and *'teflon-coated'* irons to reduce the likelihood of drying out your strands. Do note that the plates on these irons will eventually develop build-up from the impurities in water and from dried hair cells. Do pay close attention to these changes and discard your iron when it starts sticking to the hairs.

Using Flat or Curling Irons

- Start with almost dry hair that has been detangled and work in sections.
- Always apply a heat protectant to each section first.
- Move from the roots to the tips of the hair. (Don't go too close to the scalp as burns can occur!)
- Gently glide the iron down the section—no tugging or pulling.
- Avoid repeating this on each section more than twice—the possibility of heat damage increases
- Try the *chase method*—using a brush or comb to go before the flat iron to ease tangles and speed up the straightening process.

Rules for Using Heated Hair Tools

- When blow-drying, always use with the 'cool' setting. It may take 10-15 more minutes to finish, but your ends will appreciate the consideration.
- Never use a heated appliance on dirty hair (hair with a lot of product build-up).
- Flat iron on the lowest heat that will do the job.

- Try to make only one pass of a flat iron through your hair—gliding the iron down each section once only.
- *Avoid* using two forms of heat styling back-to-back: for example, blow-drying and then flat ironing.
- If you *do* use two forms of heat, remember to add a heat protectant between them as extra protection.
- Never use heat on your hair on consecutive days. Minimise to weekly use at the most—though monthly is even better!

Low-heat Styling

This usually involves setting your hair with rollers and sitting under a hooded dryer. Many women who have taken up the low-heat styling option have reaped the results they always wanted: straight hairstyles with retained length. By being gentler on the ends of your hair, you will notice the same too.

I understand that not everyone can afford to go to the salon monthly or buy a standing hood dryer. I do not expect you to do either of those things. A tabletop hood dryer is an inexpensive tool that you can also quickly store out of the way when not in use (space-saving). They can also double as a safe heat source when you are deep conditioning your hair (over a plastic cap).

I'm now going to highlight some commonly used forms of indirect or low-heat styling options.

Roller Setting

Roller setting the hair only requires you to buy rollers and pins from the beauty supply store and part the hair carefully. Most people have used rollers at one time or another for a quick curly style.

When choosing rollers, it is important to choose smooth or foam-covered rollers. Avoid Velcro (Mesh) rollers or those with small spikes as these can snag the hair and lead to breakage when being removed from the hair. Magnetic rollers with Snap-On covers are a safe bet.

The steps for roller setting one's hair are outside of the remit of this book, but you can find numerous examples online. With practise, you will get better and faster at setting your hair on rollers. The main rule is to *not roll the hair too tightly*.

Sitting under a dryer for an hour or more is tedious at the best of times, so I suggest you to prepare well. Have a book or a few magazines handy and don't forget to keep a cool drink close by.

I don't recommend sleeping with rollers though sometimes this is necessary. Foam-covered rollers are more comfortable for sleep but are not very gentle on the hair ends. Satin pillow rollers—satin covering the foam—seem to be almost perfect for overnight application. I say 'almost perfect' because there is still some tension on your roots whilst you move in your sleep.

Heated Curlers

'Heated curlers' are similar to the conventional rollers but have their own heat within them. These are ideal for use on freshly washed or clean, dry hair. As with any form of heated hair appliance, overuse will lead to dryness. Philip Kingsley recommends 'steam-producing, thermostatically controlled' heated rollers. These are infinitely better for your ends than going over them with a curling iron.

I have used the steam-producing rollers in the past with good results. I will own that the curls only lasted a few hours for me. If using these between hair washes, it is generally recommended that you protect your ends with tissue paper before applying the rollers. I always use endpapers whenever I am applying them.

Alternatives to using rollers include straw sets (using straws), perm-rod sets, flexi-rod sets, and curlformer sets. See below for pictures of the tools for these.

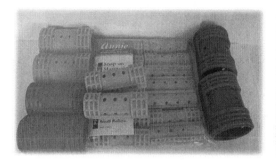 

Magnetic snap-on rollers Perm rods

Double-prong clips for rollers

Heat-free Styling

This is a concept that is close to my heart. After dabbling with heat a few times after I started my hair journey, I decided to stop and have not looked back since.

First, I want to introduce the term 'air-drying'. This just means leaving your hair to dry in the style you've chosen at ambient temperature. Hair can reshape to a new style as the moisture leaves the strands. Why? Wet hair is saturated with water, which temporarily overcomes the hydrogen bonds between the proteins. As the hair dries, these reform.

Obviously, this process takes much longer at room temperature than sitting under a hood dryer or blow-drying. Hence, to start air-drying, you must give yourself plenty of time to allow your hair to dry.

You can air-dry your hair in a variety of styles or sets. You can roller set, straw set (using straws or perm rods), braid, or twist your hair.

How to Air Dry Your Hair

1. Start with freshly washed and conditioned hair.
2. Divide your hair into 4 sections and use sectioning clips to secure.
3. Apply your leave-in conditioner and seal this into the first section with your chosen oil.
4. In each section, using a rat-tail comb, part a smaller section of hair.
5. Detangle, then braid or twist this section of hair to 1-2 inches from the ends.
6. You can either leave this as it is or apply a perm rod to the end.
7. Braid and set the remaining sections.
8. Leave hair to dry, hanging down for four or more hours.
9. Once hair is completely dry, apply some oil to your fingers and undo each section.
10. Use your fingers to lift the hair from the roots to hide the parts in your hair.

The same principle works with roller set hair. You simply roll each smaller section, secure, and allow the hair to dry. Keep a spray bottle of water handy to keep the sections from drying before you roll them. When you are done, cover with a hair net or your satin scarf and get busy around the house. (I'm not confident enough to leave the house with 'big roller head' but more power to you if you are!)

For ladies with relaxed hair who want straight hair whilst air-drying:

1. Divide freshly conditioned hair into 4 sections.
2. Moisturise and seal each section.
3. Wrap a satin scarf over your hair firmly (not tightly) and let your hair hang down the back.
4. Every 30 minutes, smooth the hair downwards with your hands until it dries.

The satin scarf will smooth out and flatten the edges of your hair, and the bulk of your hair will dry quite straight.

Learning Points from Week Five

- Using heated hair tools can speed up the development of split ends and breakage.
- Reducing your use of heated tools to special occasions only is a good start.
- Always use a 'heat protectant' styling product before using any form of heated appliance.
- The use of indirect heat or heat-free styling techniques will make a marked difference to your hair's health.
- Air-drying is the perfect way to dry your hair—retains moisture and prevents over-manipulation of the strands.

Action Plan for Week Five

- Try out a heat-free style this week: I suggest a braid-out or twist-out—unless you are an old hand with rollers.
- If you have natural hair, I suggest leaving your braids or twists in overnight to fully dry.
- Each night, simply cover your style with a satin scarf or bonnet.
- After 4 nights, section your hair into 4 and loosely braid or twist each in a big braid.
- In the morning, take down the braids and carry out your daily moisture routine.

WEEK SIX:

Detangling Your Hair

I hope you enjoyed your first foray into heat-free styling last week. You survived it!

Now for something that *a lot* of hair professionals stumble at: *detangling your hair*. Who doesn't have a childhood memory of your hair being 'tough' and many hair-styling sessions ending in tears? Or being told you are 'too tender-headed'?

With so many products and hair tools promising to rid you of your tangles, it's no wonder there is so much misinformation out there. Of course, no head of hair is the same; however, there are some principles which, when correctly applied, will yield a tear-free—and hair-yanking-free—detangling session.

Hair Myth #5: 'I Just Need One Great Product and My Hair Will Grow Long'

This myth is propagated by the haircare industry and their promises with each new product line. Of course, with research, products are becoming better tailored to our Afro-Caribbean hair types. However, hair products marketed for the Caucasian population usually work just as well for our hair. I can testify to this!

Furthermore, a more expensive product does not necessarily mean it has better ingredients than a cheaper one. And if the cheaper one is working well, why change it?

I will grant you that some organic ingredients are harder to source, and this may be reflected in the price. Nonetheless, it is entirely up to you to decide whether you want to pay the extra money for them. I believe a hair journey should not empty out your bank account but should instead be cost-effective.

Now back to detangling those tresses.

Why do we need to detangle our hair anyway?

Hair Science

As noted above, hair goes through three phases in its growth cycle. Shedding is inevitable in each hair's life cycle. In its place, another hair starts growing from the follicles after the shed hairs have detached fully from the scalp. As Afro-textured hair is not naturally straight, *shed hairs have a tendency to wrap around other strands* on their way down.

Another reason our shed hairs may not be able to make their way down are *our styling preference.* These include braids, cornrows, twists, weaves, and curly sets. You have probably noticed that when hair is left in single braids or twists for a while, the roots can start to look matted. This is from the build-up of shed hairs (and dust) as the weeks go by. Textured hairs can also lock around themselves. As 50-150 hairs can be shed daily, we definitely need to remove those shed strands from our hair.

Another reason we get tangles is due to *exposure to the elements.* Even a straight head of hair will become tangled after being out on a windy day or having a wool scarf wrapped around it. This is because the wind whips up the hair and causes friction. This friction causes the cuticles of each hair to interlock and the hairs to wrap around each other haphazardly. Hairs can also literally knot around themselves—like a knot in a rope. Disentangling the

Hairs from these knots have led many people to pull and break hairs.

The Importance of Proper Detangling

When hair is improperly handled, you are more prone to getting split ends forming. This constant wear and tear is called 'weathering'. (Dealing with split ends is discussed in week eight.) This makes your hair very vulnerable to breaking.

There are two main instances improperly handled hair will most likely break: when hair is very dry (parched) and when hair is soaking wet.

When hair is very dry, it is unable to stretch and bend with styling; hence, it breaks easily. *When hair is wet*, the water molecules overcome the hydrogen bonds, and this makes us misjudge the elasticity of our hair. The wet hairs also tend to stick to each other, making them more likely to be overstretched and break.

So how do you start detangling properly?

Tools You Will Need

- *Patience*: you need to have at least 30 minutes free, or you will rush to your hair's detriment.
- A wide-toothed comb.
- (Optional) a detangling brush (Tangle Teezer or Denman Brush).
- Sectioning clips—to keep detangled sections set apart until you are ready to style.
- A detangling spray or leave-in conditioner.

How to Detangle Your Hair

I will give you two routines for when you have textured styles or straight (or relaxed) hair.

Detangling Straight Hair

1. Gently section your hair into 4-8 parts using your fingers and secure with clips.
2. Apply your detangling spray or leave-in (a dime-size) to the first section.
3. Starting 2-3 inches from the ends of the hair, comb down with a wide-tooth comb.
4. Whenever you encounter a tangle, go just below it and comb down.
5. Move up again in a smaller jump and comb gently down (don't tug).
6. Once the tangle is loosened, comb all the way down and start a few inches further up the section.
7. Repeat until hair is tangle-free from root to ends of hair.
8. Do the same for the remainder of the hair.

Detangling Textured Hair

1. Start with damp hair (either after deep conditioning or spray with some water).
2. Section hair into 4-8 sections using your finger and secure using clips.
3. Starting 2-3 inches from the ends, comb downwards with a wide-tooth comb.
4. On finding a tangle, move below it and try combing down again.
5. If the tangle seems strongly knotted, put down the comb and use your fingers to pull strands out of it from above, gently.
6. Once loosened, pick up the comb and carry on downwards.
7. Work your way up the section.
8. (Optional) Once you can comb all the way down, repeat steps 3-7 with a detangling brush.
9. Move on to the next section and repeat steps 3-7.

How often should I be detangling my hair?

Too much of anything is bad—it's a common saying, but it's true!

For most ladies, *once a week* is plenty. With natural hair, you may even extend it to every 2-4 weeks in certain styles.

However, if you have already detangled once but unexpectedly end up with wind-blown hair, then do go over those tresses again. The once-weekly rule is waived for protective styles lasting a month or two as you cannot easily get to your hair. Since you are not manipulating the hair with the style, you are doing well.

Suggested Detangling Leave-in Conditioners

- Organics (African Pride) Leave-in Hair Mayonnaise.
- Water and aloe vera juice mix (4 parts water and one part aloe vera juice).
- Water and glycerine mix (4 parts water and one part glycerine).
- Coconut oil: a great detangler that I find softens my hair and strengthens it at the same time.

Other Detangling Considerations

As I said before, one size does not fit all! We all have different hair types and textures. For this reason, you may find that as your hair grows longer, one way of detangling does not work as well as before. Two alternatives are: in the shower or using only your fingers (no combs!).

For *shower detangling*, start under a stream of running water with hair that is saturated with a moisturising instant conditioner. Go through the hair in sections. For shoulder-length straight hair, 2-4 sections will suffice, but with natural hair, 6-8 sections will work better.

With *finger detangling*, you start at the root of each section and gently part the hair into smaller sub-sections. Then you try to gently rake your fingers down the length of your hair. If you encounter a tangle, you stop the raking motion and use your fingers to gently tease strands out of the knot. Then resume the raking until you can go from root to ends. This is not for the *faint-hearted*!

Experiment with these two only *once you have a hang of the basic detangling routines.*

The longer your hair gets, the longer your detangling sessions will take. You will probably want to style your hair in a way to minimise tangles. Hint: see you in week seven—protective-styling week!

Learning Points for Week Six

- Detangling technique is make-or-break for hair-styling routines.
- Learning how to remove shed hairs without pulling or breaking one's hair is paramount.
- Patience is the key! Give yourself time to properly comb through your hair.
- A good detangling leave-in conditioner helps but cannot replace good technique.

Action Plan for Week Six

- Choose a detangling leave-in conditioner or mix this week.
- Detangle your hair on wash day—either prior to washing your hair or after rinsing and towel drying.
- Take a look at the hairs in your comb: note down how many shed hairs there are compared to broken hairs (in your hair journal). Your aim is to reduce this over time.

Protective and Low Manipulation Styling

After laying down the foundations of healthy hair care, it naturally follows that the most effective method of realising your hair growth should also be given due mention: *protective styling*.

Protective styles are hairstyles that keep the ends of your hair tucked away from the elements. They keep the ends of your hair off your shoulders.

What are the elements that hair is being protected from?

- The *sun*: just as it can tan or burn your skin, it can weaken your hair, dry it out, and make it feel hard and stiff. Philip Kingsley (*The Hair Bible*) believes that the change in hair colour 'that the sun gives . . . is just as damaging as applying bleach!'
- The *wind*: this can whip your hair into frenzy, causing the cuticles to rub and snag against each other. This invariably leads to tangles and knots.
- *Heat or temperature changes*: in winter, as we move from dry, warmed houses to cold outdoors, our hair strands swell and shrink with the changing moisture levels in the air.
- *Chlorine and salt*: during summer, the extra swimming can really ravage and strip our hair of moisture.

- *Clothing:* cotton, wool, and polyester will dry out our hairs if they are left in contact for long enough. Winter hats can cause a build-up of static electricity and thereby cause frizzing of the hair.

Low manipulation styling is the other side of the same coin—ways to style the hair in which we don't have to keep touching or handling the hair too often.

I have found, to my surprise that straight hair is not as simple to maintain as it often seems. To maintain a fresh flat iron or roller set, you may have to wrap your hair each night (in a beehive shape) or pin-curl your hair (make curl shapes around your fingers and pin it in place). This often requires quite a bit of combing and can lead to breakage if not done carefully each time.

It is also true that each time we style our hair we are speeding up that wear-and-tear effect. If you restyle daily as opposed to weekly, your ends will see splits much sooner.

Examples of low manipulation styling alternatives are braid-out or twist-out sets. Once the hair is set, all one has to do is spray daily and cover with a bonnet nightly. To refresh the style, one could re-braid mid-week. The amount of manipulation is already much lower than a straight style—only twice compared to seven times in a week.

In a protective style like a bun, you may be able to keep your bun intact for the whole week. You can wrap a scarf around it at night and spray in the mornings. The scarf will smooth the hairs overnight, making the bun look fresh for longer. The added bonus is that your ends are hidden inside the bun, away from the drying external elements.

Overleaf is a table with examples of protective and low manipulation styles.

Low manipulation styles	Protective styles
Braid-out	Box braids (with extensions added)
Twist-out	Senegalese or kinky twists
Straw set or finger coils	Cornrows
Flexi-rod set	Flat twists
Roller set	Buns and Up-dos
Afro puff	Weaves
Wash 'n' go Afro	Wigs

Here is a collage of some of my protective styles during my hair journey.

Protective Styles 1

Do I have to protective style?

No, you don't. I know several ladies who have managed to grow their hair down their backs without protective styling.

How did they do this?

They kept up a *very good moisturising routine.* By moisturising twice a daily and deep conditioning up to twice a week, their ends were better prepared to face the elements without drying out or breaking. Hence, they retained their growth and reached longer lengths without having to hide their ends all the time.

Hair Myth #6: 'Braids Will Grow Your Hair!'

Although I have seen so many examples to the contrary, it seems everyone believes this to be *gospel truth*! Just the other day, my cousin repeated this, and I had to bite my tongue.

Braids are one of the most widely accepted and used forms of protective styling among black women. From Africa to Europe and the United States, braids are swinging all over the place.

My Hair History—Part 2

As a child, I wore cornrows and braids—using only my own hair—for years. My hair would grow just past my shoulders and then break off. I loved the many styles I could wear for 2 to 4 weeks. When I became a teenager, I moved to UK, and the cold weather meant I would need to do box braids with extensions.

Even now I can remember that once, as a 5-year-old, my mum had gotten me braids with extensions. My scalp had itched so badly, I actually wanted to be bald! We had travelled down to visit my grandparents in the village so I had to keep that hairstyle for a while. Torture! It was shortly after this incident that I was given my first relaxer.

As a teenager, I became the braid queen. My first set of braids—though I had asked for medium-sized braids—were too small and tight. Everywhere I went, a strand of braids would fall out—with my roots in it! It was very embarrassing to have people—at a predominantly white school—handing me my braids knowingly. Obviously, we didn't call that braider again!

I would get braids every 3 months—to last the school term—and at the end, my hair would be a dry, frizzy mess! My hair *never* even got past shoulder length in those 5 years. Once, as a senior, I got a weave. I looked so different I kept double taking in the mirror! I would go back and get more weaves until I was halfway through my university degree.

That was when I discovered the Crown and Glory Method™. A friend of mine—who had been styling her hair in its natural texture for most of her life—led me to the site: www.growafrohairlong. com.

It seemed this was what I had been looking for!

A braid regimen—with video tutorials on how to add extensions myself—and hair growth! I was so inspired by the pictures on the site; I quickly installed my own single braids—okay, installing them actually took me three days—and started the regime. I even bought one of the products from the site.

Two years later, I still had shoulder-length hair. Why? This was simply because my hair was still dry when I took it down, and I did not have a deep-conditioning routine. Furthermore, I still didn't know how to care for my own hair outside of extension styles!

Once I was taking better care of my hair *out of braids*, I was able to take *great care* of my hair whilst in braids. The lesson is this:

Until you know how to gently handle your hair daily, don't hide it away for months in the hopes that you'll suddenly have waist-length locks.

Braids, like many other practices, can make or break your hair. In the wrong hands, your hair can really suffer.

The Downside of Braids

With the wrong braider, you can have the problem I had with my first set as a teenager. At 13, I should not have been experiencing hair loss! Very small sections with heavy extension hair *will* rip out your strands. If the braids are too tight, your follicles will suffer for it. *Traction alopecia*—the term for hair loss related to too tight hair maintenance practices—is a **very real** possibility at any age!

If this abuse continually happens, the hair follicles may not recover, and the hairs in those areas may stop growing back. Thankfully, this did not happen to me but many have not been so fortunate.

I have also noted that the most popular hair extensions for installing braids are the synthetic fibres such as Kanekalon and Toyokalon. These fibres can have a drying effect on our strands. Human hair will reduce this tendency, but if you are regularly braiding, this may not be as cost-effective—think of the student purse.

The last downside is the matted roots you can get after a few weeks to a month of having single braids installed.

The main ways to combat these issues are to ensure you enlist a good braider who will not pull your hair too tightly and have a regular cleansing and moisture routine. The synthetic fibres will still allow you to spray on your daily moisturiser. Finally, I stress: *avoid do micro braids (tiny braids)*. You've been warned!

Hair Care in Protective Styles

Whether you are choosing braids, twists, or weaves, you need to have a daily and weekly routine. Follow the daily moisture routine of week 3 but incorporate these:

Cleansing Techniques

- You can wash your braids, but I suggest using diluted cleanser to reduce build-up at the roots.
- Cleanse your tresses weekly or biweekly.
- If in a weave, dilute your cleanser, then spray on to your roots, massage, and rinse well.
- Never go to bed with a wet weave (mildew is a real concern).
- Lightly oil your scalp after cleansing your braids or twists or weaves—oil applicator bottles are good.

Moisturising Techniques

- Moisturise your braids or twists daily with a moisturising spray mix. Oil sheen is a nice sealant!
- Spray the roots of your weave with a moisture mix.
- Cover your hair at night with a satin bonnet or scarf—it will keep your style neater for longer.
- If you are wearing a bun, a spray or a lotion for moisturising will do equally well.

How to Take Down Protective Styles

This is by far the most daunting part of any protective style. You thought you looked good with your style, and now it is time to unravel and reveal your tresses: the moment of truth.

Well, I will give you a short but simple set of takedown routines for each protective-style.

Takedown for Single Braids or Twists

1. Spray a section of your braids with a moisture mix.
2. Snip the ends of the braids below your hair length using a pair of scissors (look for the change in hair colour as your hair tapers in the braid).
3. Start undoing the braid gently. You can use the rat-tail end of a comb by that name.
4. Once you've loosened and removed around 8-10 braids, spray them with aloe vera juice, apply a thumb-size of coconut oil to that section and twist it up loosely.
5. Repeat until you are done. Take plenty of water and rest breaks.
6. Undo each twist and detangle using the textured detangling routine.
7. Apply some protein treatment to each section before re-twisting. You can join up two sections if you prefer.
8. Carry on with a wash-day routine after your protein treatment.
9. Detangle briefly afterwards and style.

Takedown Routine for Weaves

1. Sit facing a mirror and find the thread of the weave.
2. Using a pair of scissors carefully cut the thread. It should unravel for a few turns.
3. Loosen the weft and search for the next piece of thread to cut until all wefts are removed.
4. Find the end of the braided cornrow.
5. Spray the braided hair with a moisture mix and start to unravel.
6. Once all the hair is loosened, section hair into 8 sections and spray each with aloe vera juice or apply a thumb-size of coconut oil. Twist up each section.
7. Now untwist one section at a time, detangle (textured routine), and apply protein treatment before re-twisting.
8. Continue with wash-day routine and detangle briefly after deep conditioning.

Takedown Routine for Buns and Up-dos (Left in for More Than Five Days)

1. Spray hair with moisture mix.
2. Carefully remove hairpins and hair elastics.
3. Remove any bun inserts carefully.
4. Spray aloe vera juice on hair and part into 4 sections.
5. Apply coconut oil and leave on for 20-30 minutes under a plastic cap.
6. Rinse and carry on with your wash-day cleansing and deep conditioning.
7. Detangle in sections afterwards—follow either textured or straight techniques depending on your hair type when dry.

Learning Points for Week Seven

- Protective and low manipulation styles protect your hair ends from the elements or manipulation.
- They can make a vast difference in how well you retain your hair's length.

- Following a moisturising and cleansing routine during each style is as important as the style itself.
- How you take down your protective style will determine whether you experience breakage or not.

Action Plan for Week Seven

- Write down your previous protective styles and list their pros and cons—for you.
- Choose a short-term protective style: bun, up-do, twists, or braids on your own hair.
- Try it out on your hair after completing your wash-day routine.
- After one week, take down the protective style carefully.
- Write down your thoughts: was it hard to keep your hair in that protective style? Did you settle into the daily routine easily? Would you want to do the same style again?
- See you next week (you're almost there)!

WEEK EIGHT:

Going the Distance and Hair Journey Tools

When I embarked on my healthy hair journey in July 2008, I did believe my hair could get longer. I just didn't imagine it could reach the lengths it has! The best thing is that even when I stop looking for growth, my new habits allow me to keep realising growth. I keep retaining the ends of my hair and, thereby, am reaching new lengths.

I want you to remember that my hair has grown with consistent care, not because I made a *drastic* change! I was still relaxing my hair regularly for the first year and a half of my hair journey. I was still flat ironing my hair in the first year of my journey. I simply added in some healthier practices and reduced the more damaging ones as time went on. My hair grew down the middle of my back with relaxers still in the mix!

Why am I pointing this out? It's simple. Hair is hair! You *can* have *healthy relaxed hair* and you can have *healthy natural hair*. The main differences are the styling options and your routine for making it more manageable for your lifestyle. With any hairstyle, you need to make it work for you, not the other way round!

Keeping straight hair requires ingenuity—not to have constant fly-aways or bends in the hair from ponytail holders. Similarly, textured hair can tend to frizz with the wrong hair tools and techniques.

I simply decided during my hair journey that I had sufficiently mastered my relaxed hair and wanted to master my hair in its natural state. After all, with the correct care, I could safely achieve straight styles when I wanted to. This extra flexibility of natural hair—not to mention the thickness I had always craved—was enough to lure me!

I don't want you to think you need to stop relaxing your hair. Neither do I want you to start relaxing your hair to see length (another popular hair myth). You will see length with patience and perseverance with any hair style or type.

Hair-length retention is the main aim of these efforts, and having a regimen is a means to achieve this. It's exactly like having a workout schedule or routine to achieve your toning or weight loss goals!

Now I am going to share a few more techniques you can fit into your weekly or monthly regimens to really bolster your efforts so far.

Co-washing

Co-washing is *cleansing your hair with a conditioner in place of a shampoo*. This gets your scalp clean through the fingertip-scalp massage. Furthermore, conditioner has milder surfactants in it than shampoo but is still able to clean the hair by clinging on to the dirt and allowing it to rinse off. The final benefit is the conditioning and moisture it infuses into hair at the same time it is being cleansed!

I decided within the first few months of my hair journey to supplement my regimen with a co-wash mid-week and found that my hair was softer as a result. I completely removed shampoos from my regimen after six months, and my hair has thrived without them. You don't have to cut out shampooing but it's good to know it is an option.

How to Co-wash

1. Divide hair into 4-8 sections and secure with a clip.
2. Wet hair under a shower and squeeze out excess water.
3. Apply a palm-sized amount of conditioner to each section from roots to ends.
4. Apply half the amount to the scalp and massage well with fingertips (not nails).
5. Rinse each section once with warm water and then repeat application of conditioner.
6. Leave conditioner on for 3-5 minutes whilst bathing and then rinse well.
7. Squeeze excess water out and gently dry with a towel or T-shirt.

You do not need to follow a co-wash with a deep condition if it is done mid-week. If it is done on wash day, I do recommend you to continue with your deep condition. Your hair will feel softer after the second rinse and even air-dried hair will be noticeably smoother. Some ladies use a different conditioner for each rinse. Other women do three rinses; however, this is not necessary.

It is important to note that as many conditioners contain silicones, you can get product build-up with repeated use of these. Therefore, clarifying your hair monthly would still be highly recommended.

Suggested Co-washing Conditioners

- Herbal Essences Hello Hydration conditioner
- Tresemme Naturals Vibrantly Smooth Conditioner
- Tresemme Naturals Nourishing Moisture Conditioner
- Giovanni Tea-Tree Tingle Conditioner

I have found that most instant conditioners are very good for co-washing with. The main exceptions to this rule are the conditioners which have protein in them. These can start to make one's hair feel hard after a few rinses. I quickly noted this but once I selected mainly moisturising conditioners, my hair was back to loving the experience of co-washing.

Pre-poo

A *pre-poo* is an abbreviation for a *pre-shampoo conditioning treatment*.

This is very beneficial to our Afro-textured hair types, which often tend to be made drier by shampoos. A *pre-poo* is done by adding a conditioning treatment or some natural oils to the hair before shampooing and subsequent conditioning. This helps to boost the moisture levels in the hair prior to shampooing and reduces the removal of the natural oils on our strands.

How to Pre-poo

1. Start with dry or damp hair.
2. Divide hair into 4-8 sections and secure with clips or in braids or twists.
3. Starting at the ends of the hair, apply your conditioning treatment or oils to each section.
4. Finally, apply it to the hair at the roots and cover hair with a plastic cap.
5. Leave for 30-40 minutes (or overnight, like I do) and rinse hair with warm water.
6. Apply a quarter palm-size of shampoo or cleanser to each section at the roots.
7. Massage the roots well and rinse well under stream of water.
8. Follow with your deep-conditioning routine or an instant conditioner.

The reason you can often forego a deep conditioner after a pre-poo is if you used a moisturising deep conditioner in the pre-treatment. Using moisturising oils like olive oil or sunflower oil also allow you to waive your post-wash deep condition. If you use a protein-based treatment as your initial pre-poo, though, you will need to finish with a moisturising deep conditioner to soften and smoothe your hair. Suggested pre-poos include the natural oils, moisturising deep conditioners, and protein treatments listed above in weeks 1, 3 and 4.

A lot of women swear by pre-pooing for their increased moisture levels, and I usually find that this is my default mode of deep conditioning as I tend to do it overnight.

Baggying

Baggying is applying your chosen daily moisturiser and then covering your hair with a plastic bag to allow your scalp heat to let the moisturiser absorb better. The bag can be left on for 30 minutes, a few hours or even overnight. For overnight treatments, you apply a bit more than the usual amount. When you are ready to take off the 'baggy', you simply apply your sealing oil, style, and go.

This technique has been recently updated to the 'GHE' or 'green house effect', which involves applying several layers of hats and coverings to ensure the head heats up promptly. This is said to enhance the effect as well as stimulate the production of sebum. The truth of the latter claim is still yet to be proven, but the moisturising benefits are more than obvious.

The 'baggy' is usually a plastic cap, sandwich bag, or even cling film. This can be applied to the entire head or just over a ponytail or bun. The latter two options allow you to focus the moisture on the ends of the hair where it is most needed.

Trimming or Dusting Your Hair

'Dusting' is when you conduct a very light trim on the ends of your hair. This is usually to the tune of $1/8^{th}$ to ¼ of an inch of hair clipped from the ends of the hair. This is done in small sections and allows you to keep split ends under control and at bay.

This also allows you not to undergo routine trims as they will be unnecessary with this regular practice. Dusting can be done every month, every few months, or even more regularly. I advise you don't do it more often than every 3 weeks though. Any closer together and you may actually be accumulating a haircut over time!

Dusting is simple but needs the correct equipment. You need haircutting scissors, which can usually be bought at a beauty supply store or even the chemists. Next, I recommend you to ensure you have time to do your whole head or at least half in a session.

Trimming, on the other hand takes ½ to a whole inch off the hair ends each time (if not a bit more).

How to Trim Your Ends

1. Section hair into 4 sections, have a mirror in front of you with good lighting above.
2. Start with one section, take a quarter of the section, and pull them straight.
3. Are the ends even? Are there hairs any sticking straight past?
4. Cut only ¼ of an inch off the longest pieces. (These are lead hairs—the rest will catch up in time.)
5. Look at the ends of the rest of that section, any thinner or splitting ends.
6. Trim just above the splits on individual strands and comb that piece again.
7. Look at the ends again and trim any splits you can see.
8. Move on to the next quarter and repeat steps 2-7.
9. *Alternately*, in step 2, two strands twist the quarter section and snip the ends of the twist (1/4 inch maximum).

Search and Destroy Method

1. Ensure you have good lighting and have a piece of blank white paper in front of you for contrast (either on your lap or propped up facing you).
2. Pick small sections of your hair and twist it anticlockwise from roots to ends.
3. Different lengths of your hair will stick out of the section.
4. Look at the ends and identify split ends using the chart in week 4.
5. Cut just above the split ends.
6. Pick other sections and repeat the above steps all over your head.

This method takes a lot of time and patience, but you will be rid of split ends without losing your hair length.

Stretching (for the Relaxed Ladies Only)

Stretching is the term used to describe the practice of prolonging the time between routine relaxer touch-ups. Instead of relaxing your new growth every eight weeks, waiting until ten or twelve weeks between services. This allows your hair to grow out and prevents the common problem of overprocessing the hair.

Overprocessing occurs when the relaxer is either left on a section of untreated hair for too long or when a previously treated section has relaxer reapplied to it in error. The relaxer continues to break the protein bonds in the hair and this leads to a weakness that makes hair very prone to breakage. The point where new growth meets relaxed hair is known as *the line of demarcation*. This is where the hair is most likely to break with regular combing or styling due to the change in texture and characteristics of the hair.

With more than one inch of new growth, it is easier for the stylist to correctly apply the relaxer to the new growth only. Another way to further protect previously processed strands of hair is to apply an oil or conditioner to the hair above the demarcation line. This will slow down the processing of any relaxer applied slightly above this line.

I do not advise that you decide to stretch your hair for a longer period than you are already used to as your first attempt. I suggest going for nine weeks initially and then ten weeks the next time.

This way, you will learn to blend the new growth and relaxed ends in styles from week six post-relaxer touch-up. Great styles for this time include braid-outs, twist-outs, and curly sets like roller sets and Bantu knot-outs.

I strongly discourage the use of direct heat to straighten the new growth as your only mode of blending the textures. Direct-heat styling can significantly weaken the whole hair strand.

Another tip: *don't neglect your protein treatments*. Protein will strengthen the demarcation line, thereby reducing the chances of breakage.

Stretching became much easier for me the further I was in my healthy hair journey and meant I could take the plunge to transition when I was finally ready to. When I first learned about stretching, I immediately attempted a six-month stretch! Needless to say, I got a lot of breakage! You live and you learn.

Learning Points for Week Eight

- There are other techniques to further boost your hair's moisture levels and enhance your length retention.
- Regular dusting can be done in lieu of trims to keep a close eye on split ends.
- Ladies with relaxers (and other chemical processes) can go a bit longer between touch-ups to prevent their previously processed strands from overprocessing.

Action Plan for Week Eight

- Do another protein treatment before your cleansing routine on wash day (as a pre-poo).
- Try either a mid-week co-wash or baggy treatment.
- Write down how your hair feels immediately after and a day afterwards.
- Write down your hair current regimen including how often you moisturise and seal, how often you wash and deep condition, and how often you do a protein treatment.
- Next to each step write down the names of your chosen cleanser, deep conditioner, moisturiser, protein treatment, and oil for sealing.

That Extra Mile and Research

In this chapter, I will talk about the additional considerations when embarking on and continuing a successful healthy hair journey. These include the impact of nutrition, health, and lifestyle on your hair. The most important thing I will be discussing at the end is: research: continually increasing your hair education! Shall we begin?

Hair growth and the quality of the hair we are growing are very much linked to the amount of nutrition and the state of health of the body from which it stems. I will tackle nutrition first.

You have probably heard the saying, 'You are what you eat.' Whilst this is not universally applicable, with hair, you only get back what you put in. We have so far dwelt on the external measures to retain the hair we grow. Now I will discuss the importance of ensuring there are adequate nutrients supplying the follicles.

Hair Science

Nutrition and Your Hair Growth

Hair receives its nutrients and oxygen supply from the capillary bed within the scalp. Hair grows quite quickly—in spite of appearances—being the second fastest reproducing tissue in the body (the first is bone marrow). Hair does grow 1/50th of an inch every day.

Hair and nails, however, are not ranked as the most 'essential' tissues in the body. Hence, nutrients are given in preference to other more 'vital' organs before the hair and nails see them. It makes sense, therefore, that one often notices deficiencies in the diet in both the hair and nails first. After all, the nutrients available will be diverted to the vital organs.

For instance, a dietary deficiency of iron can lead to brittle nails with vertical stripes. In this condition, hair is often dry, dull, and brittle with an increased tendency to shed.

By ensuring that your diet has all the essential food groups, you will be guaranteeing that your hair is growing at its optimal rate and is a better, stronger grade of hair.

Essential 'Hair Food'

As aforementioned, hair is mainly made up of protein. Therefore, you must ensure you are getting enough protein in your diet to allow production of new hair at the follicles. Furthermore, getting your multivitamins—especially B vitamins—will enhance energy release from the food you consume. Other essential minerals include iron (as mentioned above) and zinc. Iron is important for the creation of haemoglobin in the blood which carries oxygen to all the tissues. Zinc is important for cell and protein synthesis (production).

It is recommended that you ensure you eat a portion of protein at least twice a day—each portion is roughly two to three ounces or a deck of cards. Furthermore, ensure you get your five fruit and vegetable portions daily. I know many people struggle with five portions, so I suggest a daily multivitamin and mineral tablet until you get up to speed.

Zinc is a trace mineral so you only need small amounts daily. Even a slight deficiency will be noticed by your hair. Dietary sources of zinc include red meat, poultry, shell fish, whole grains, and dairy products. Do note that the amounts of zinc available from the vegetable forms are lower than animal sources. Iron can be found in red meat and green leafy vegetables, though vegetable forms need Vitamin C (ascorbic acid) for optimum absorption.

Health and Your Hair

Another important factor in hair growth and the strength of your hair is your general well-being. There are a host of medical conditions that can cause hair loss, hair shedding, or hair breakage. However, one cannot overlook the obvious. Just as malnutrition can cause hair breaking and loss, stress and lack of regular exercise can set back a hair journey.

Stress is a well-recognised cause of sudden hair shedding or loss. It is important to pay attention to any sources of undue stress in your life if you start experiencing such symptoms.

Exercise is an important factor for heart, lungs, skin and hair health! With it, all your organs function better owing mainly to better oxygenation and delivery of nutrients (from the heart-boosting effects). I will admit (both hands up) that my hair journey also re-kindled my health journey.

I will briefly discuss two conditions which can cause your hair to be growing at a sub-optimal rate or even cause hair loss.

Iron deficiency anaemia is the first, and as mentioned above, this can leave one with dry, brittle strands that seem to find even minor styling too much of a challenge. Lethargy, fatigue, and pallor (pale skin) are other accompanying signs of this. A quick visit to the doctor with appropriate blood tests will tell you whether your iron intake needs to be supplemented or not. There are other causes for iron deficiency outside of diet, but knowledge of the condition is the first step to correctly diagnosing the cause and effective treatment.

The second condition encompasses the functioning of the thyroid gland. The thyroid gland is a very important tissue in regulating the body's metabolism. An underactive or overactive thyroid can both cause hair loss. With an underactive thyroid, weight gain, lethargy, and dry skin are accompanying features. With an overactive thyroid, weight loss, anxiety, and restlessness are presenting symptoms. With prompt diagnosis (blood testing) and correct treatment, the hair loss can be halted and reversed.

In spite of the above conditions, one can still achieve longer hair with proper haircare practices, geared towards gentle handling of the strands.

Research and Your Hair Journey

When I use the word, 'research', I am not speaking of laboratory tests and multinational studies on hair and products. I am speaking about an individual's motivation to continually learn more about one's hair. I would be remiss if I told you all these things and didn't tell you to do your own background work.

A healthy hair journey is a personal one. No one can do it for you! You decide when to start and stop. You decide whether your efforts are worth it. For this reason, I want you to remain open to information about healthy haircare practices that could take your journey to the next level.

I initially had an aborted hair journey 2 years before my current one—see My Hair History Part 2 in Week 7—because the information I had was still lacking certain *vital* elements. Mainly, it was missing a *consistent routine* for taking care of my hair. I also did not fully understand each technique I was trying out.

Thankfully, I did not give up and neither should you. *Your hair is a part of the first impression you make, and it is a source of pride when your hair is flourishing (and others notice it).*

For that reason, I encourage you to continue finding out more about your hair—not just from trying out techniques or products at home but by going online and interacting with other women on hair journeys. Social networking sites have really taken off with many women supporting each other on their haircare journeys. On these sites, I was inspired by the progress of other women who started where I did.

There are also forums where people will share their experiences, triumphs, and setbacks with certain styles, products, or practices. Sometimes, personal experience is too harsh a way to learn! By engaging with these ladies, you can learn without going through the heartache (or emptying out your purse).

In Appendix, I have listed a few websites which are great starting points for hair journeys. Although I was a member on most of these, I did not start utilising their full resources until I was past a year into my hair journey. I say this to reassure you in case you feel overwhelmed by the information out there. I started my searches online but later bought one or two books on hair care. Buying the books gave me tangible, readily available resources to dip into at home.

Trial and Error

The first eight weeks have been giving the basics of a healthier hair journey with tried and tested practices. As mentioned above, there will be other newer techniques that will work to varying degrees. I do not want you to immediately turn a blind eye to these. I just want you to make informed decisions.

To feel more confident about any new technique, I suggest you fully inform yourself about it. If you have only asked a few women on *one site* or checked the FAQ section only, you have not properly researched that topic. This is your hair in question so I strongly advise you against taking any drastic steps without sufficient information on each new practice.

Since I was initially still having my hair regularly relaxed, I researched how to detangle, wash, moisturise, and, eventually, relax my hair at home. With each new technique, I would search threads and forums online for more in-depth explanations and guidance before I embarked on them.

From these searches, I put together an A4 ring-binder folder in which I catalogued new facts and tips I had printed out for future use. This is a great way to keep things close to hand. (And yes, I am a hair geek!) It also means you are not always relying on the Internet connection when you are trying to quickly jog your memory.

The only caution I will offer is to *avoid trying* every *new technique of the month*! These are also called 'bandwagons'. They involve a number of people trying out a certain new product or technique together without very adequate proof of any efficacy. The main problem with a bandwagon is that the unwanted side effects only become apparent after everyone is on-board. Instead of one head of hair being affected, several tales of woe unfold.

Instead, I suggest you to give your hair a break once you have a new technique that is beneficial. Continue them for at least 2 months before adding anything else to the routine.

You and Your Hairdresser

I am not suggesting that you never visit a salon again. Instead, I am trying to help you take an active role in your hair's health and growth journey. That way, your hairdresser will be a *partner* on your journey.

That being said, I have heard of and I have had a few worrisome experiences at the salon.

However, being an informed customer will free you from the helpless feeling whilst in the chair. With your routine in place, you can explain how you like your hair to be taken care of. This will prevent any setbacks on your journey from one visit.

For instance, you can ask for your hair to be steamed after your colour treatment or relaxer, prior to styling. To dry the hair, you can ask for a roller set or head wrap under a hooded dryer. For protective styles, ensure braids and cornrows are not pulled tightly during installation.

My main message is, *take charge of your hair and the salon experience will be more pleasant.*

Learning Points for Week Nine

- Nutrition is important to your hair: without the correct building blocks, you will grow more brittle hair.
- There are conditions which can affect your hair growth and retention. With correct treatment, you can still achieve your hair health and length goals.
- You must be willing to adequately research new hair practices and continually learn more about your hair.
- Your salon experiences can be empowering *and* a hair treat.

Action Points for Week Nine

- Invest in a daily multivitamin and minerals to ensure you are getting enough.
- Join a haircare social networking site to meet with other women on their hair journeys.
- **Optional:** buy a ring-binder folder and start compiling information on something about your hair journey that is still perplexing: relaxing hair, heat-free methods to straighten hair, another detangling technique etc. It really helped me.

Final Word: It's Your Journey!

'Write the vision and make it plain on tablets, that he may run who reads it.' (Habakkuk 2: 2)

Starting out on a journey is good by itself, but what really sets it apart and increases the chances of your success is *your focus and planning*. This applies to everything in life, and hair should not be any different.

The steps I have been outlining in the preceding weeks have all been part of building a haircare regimen. This book simply gives you steps to ensure you are still working towards your hair care goals daily and weekly.

I will be the first to admit that watching hair grow is like 'watching paint dry'. It can be tiresome if we are always checking every mirror and wondering: 'Has my hair grown longer?' and 'How about now?'

As I mentioned above, hair grows by half an inch every month, on average. Observing on a weekly basis will not reassure someone who is actually *on schedule*. With a weekly routine to follow, you know you are pretty much on course.

'Though it tarries, wait for it; because it will surely come, it will not tarry.' (Habakkuk 2: 3)

Consistency is the key. As you continue to repeat these techniques, they will become a habit for you. Soon, it will be almost unheard of for you to have neglected to moisturise your hair daily or protect it overnight.

A great way to keep an eye on your journey is by taking pictures along the way. This allows you to fully appreciate how far your hair has come. *I recommend taking pictures to check length every eight weeks minimum.* For styling purposes, you can take pictures weekly to chronicle the newfound versatility of your hair.

A final thought is that you should always remember that *your hair journey is unique to you.* By comparing your hair's progress to another person's, you will lose the joy of discovering just what your hair is capable of. I suggest that you take it one day at a time and you will get there.

With that said, I really appreciate you for embarking on this journey with me, and I pray you realise, every one of your goals!

Bonus—Product Ingredients

The reason I put this as an extra rather than focus a week on it is simple. Products only account for 1 per cent of healthy hair results! The other 99 per cent is the haircare techniques you regularly use. That being said, good quality products do *help* with detangling, styling, and conditioning your hair.

Here are my top seven ingredients that I search for in products before I put them in my shopping basket.

Keep an open mind.

Do consider products that are not marketed for 'black' or 'natural' hair types. Products formulated for dry, colour-treated, or damaged hair tend to be very moisturising or fortifying. Therefore, they are great for boosting the health and manageability of your hair. They may also be easier to find in grocery stores and markets.

Moisturising Ingredients

1. *Water (aqua or agua)*—what could be more moisturising?
2. *Aloe vera juice* (aloe barbadenis leaf juice)

   (a) pH 4.5-5.5: so pH balancing.
   (b) Moisturising, nourishing, and healing.

3. *Glycerine (vegetable)*

   (a) Humectant—draws moisture into hair.

4. *Panthenol (pro-vitamin B5)*

   (a) A plant derived source of Vitamin B.
   (b) Penetrates the follicle (scalp) and attracts moisture from air into hair shaft.
   (c) Creates a protective film to aid moisture retention.
   (d) Smoothes the hair: soft and silky feel.

5. *Honey*

   (a) Humectant.
   (b) Antibacterial.

Sealing Ingredients

1. *Natural oils and butters:* olive oil, coconut oil, sweet almond, jojoba—all good emollients, nourishing and protecting. Shea butter, Mango butter and Avocado butter are thicker and creamier.

Strengthening Ingredients

1. *Vegetable proteins*: silk amino acids or hydrolysed silk protein, oat protein, milk protein, soy protein, and wheat protein.

Questionable Ingredients

Consider these products carefully as they are the subjects of many (often quite heated) debates. If it works for you, go for it!

1. *Mineral oil (Paraffinum liquidum)*: a petrochemical by-product (from crude oil) that is used widely as an emollient. It works by sitting on the surface of your hair, forming a barrier that protects the hair's cuticle. This creates a smooth, flyaway free look and gives shine. It also coats the hair, working as a barrier against moisture loss and humidity.
   Unfortunately, it is comedogenic (clogs pores) and can often create a bit of 'build-up' on hair. Therefore, it is important to wash your hair a couple times a week to rid

the hair of oil and dirt build-up. These effects of mineral oil work as a topical treatment, meaning it is effective until it is washed away. However, many women have managed to keep healthy heads of hair with mineral oil-based products in their repertoire.

2. *Petrolatum (Mineral oil jelly):* this has much the same effects as mineral oil, but it is heavier and stickier. Often used as a scalp base to prevent the harsh effects of any relaxer that inadvertently touches the scalp. Some ladies have used this as a heavy sealant for the ends of their hair after moisturising. As it is a heavier form of mineral oil, it can very easily weigh down finer hair strands and cause them to stick (temporarily) together.

3. *Parabens (methyl, propyl, or butylparabens):* widely used as preservatives for their antimicrobial properties. Can cause allergic reactions and rashes if used in excess of 5 per cent level.

4. *Alcohol (ethanol, denatured alcohol, ethyl alcohol, methanol, isopropyl and SD alcohol (rubbing alcohol)):* used as carrying agents or solvents but are quite drying to hair and each could be an irritant to skin and scalp. I recommend that you do a patch test on a small section of your scalp before first full use: leave on for five minutes, rinse, and review the area after twenty-four hours to ensure no reactions. (Not to be confused with fatty alcohols which are actually fatty acids that moisturise the hair).

5. *Sodium lauryl sulphate (SLS) and sodium laureth sulphate (SLES):* mainly used in shampoos as a detergent and surfactant (sticks to dirt and oils to remove them as you rinse). It is very drying on Afro-Caribbean hair textures. It can also cause eye irritation. SLES is milder but can still be quite drying. Women who use these shampoos just ensure they use more moisturising products in between to counter these effects.

6. *Silicones:*
   Arguments against:

   • It's man-made, aka synthetic.
   • It can prevent hair from absorbing moisture.

- When these products build-up, they can weigh down the hair strands, making it appear greasy and limp.
- Silicones that do the latter include *dimethicone, alkyl and phenyl silicones.*

Arguments for:

- Some silicones *are* water soluble and do evaporate. Examples are *cyclomethicone and cyclopentasiloxane.* They are known as 'volatile' *silicones.*
- Silicones can smoothe the hair, thus aiding detangling.
- They can prevent hair from absorbing too much moisture in humid weather, thereby taming frizz-prone hair.
- Silicones coat the hair and protect it from drying out in dry weather.
- Some silicones also act as heat protectants, absorbing some of the damage and *protecting* the hair.

The choice of products is yours, but you should start to look a bit more closely at what you are regularly placing on your hair. By choosing moisture-rich products, dry hair can be transformed. By choosing which styling products to use, you can safely manage your hair—with or without the use of heat-styling appliances.

Appendix

References

Books

Hair: The Long and Short of It by Art Neufeld, 2012.

- Chapter 2: 'The Hair Itself'—information on hair density, growth rate, and hair structure.
- Chapter 3: 'Hair Growth and the Construction Zone'—hair follicles and hair growth cycle.

The Hair Bible: A Complete Guide to Health and Care by Philip Kingsley, 2003. Aurum Press Ltd.

- Chapter 14: 'Styling Your Hair Safely'—information on choosing heat-styling tools.
- Chapter 15: 'Your Health and Your Hair'—learn about how certain conditions affect hair growth and quality.
- Chapter 16: 'Hair Nutrition'—talks about supplements and even gives examples of 'perfect meals' for boosting hair health. Protein is important for hair, but there are a few surprising facts too—read about black tea and hair!
- Chapter 19: 'Frustrations and Difficulties'—discussing tangling hair and how to *gently* deal with them.
- Chapter 20: 'The Four Seasons'—learn how to ensure your hair is not ravaged by changing weather with a few recipes thrown in for DIY hair-salvaging treatments.

- Chapter 27: 'Hair Myths'—I love this chapter. There are many myths listed in this chapter, some I hadn't considered before.
- Chapter 28: 'Hair Products'—quite a comprehensive chapter that surmises that the more expensive product is not necessarily better. It's all in the labelling, read carefully before you buy.

Online Resources

Long Hair Care Forum: As I progressed on my journey, this became a great place to share and learn new tips and tricks for hair care.

- **LHCF:** www.longhaircareforum.com/

Black Hair Media: A forum for styling natural or relaxed hair with many success stories.

- **BHM:** http://forum.blackhairmedia.com/

CurlyNikki.com: A host of articles on hair health and product formulations.

- The mineral oil debate: http://www.curlynikki.com/search/label/Curly%20Hair%20Ingredients?&max-results=6
- A closer look at mineral oil: http://www.curlynikki.com/2011/10/closer-look-at-mineral-oil-natural-hair.html

Naturallycury.com: A forum where you can discuss a myriad of haircare practices and products.

- Another mineral oil debate you might enjoy: http://www.naturallycurly.com/curlreading/curl-products/mineral-oil-has-it-gotten-a-bad-rap?page=2

Find Me Online At

- Website: www.lolascurls.com
- YouTube: www.youtube.com/user/lolascrib
- Facebook: www.facebook.com/lolas.curls
- Twitter: https://twitter.com/lolascurls
- Tumblr: http://mycurlsandme.tumblr.com/
- Fotki Page: http://members.fotki.com/lolascrib/about/

Online Resources that Spurred on My Hair Journey

- YouTube (this is a very wide source and it's easy to get overwhelmed. Start with one channel at a time.)
- Fotki: www.fotki.com
- Kiss: www.keepitsimplesista.ning.com
- Hairlista: www.hairlista.com
- LHCF: www.longhaircareforum.com/
- BHM: http://forum.blackhairmedia.com/

On the above sites and forums, I found like-minded women who inspired me to keep striving to reach my hair goals with better hair practices. We would chat online, ask questions, and eventually meet up.

If you are based in the United Kingdom, do join the *UK Ladies group*: http://www.hairlista.com/group/ukladiesseekandfind to find out where we source our products and meet up with us for product swaps and journey encouragement.

I also regularly organise healthy hair workshops that allow you to learn even more about your hair and get advice in person. The blog on lolascurls.com will have details of the upcoming meet ups.

Haircare Terms: Abbreviations

Hair lengths	Haircare techniques	Natural ingredients
EL—Ear Length	DC—Deep Condition	EO—Essential Oil
CBL—Collarbone Length	CW—Conditioner Wash	
NL—Neck Length	CWC—Conditioner, Wash, Conditioner	ACV—Apple Cider Vinegar
SL—Shoulder Length	S&D—Search and Destroy (Method to Trim Spilt Ends)	SAA—Silk Amino Acid
APL—Armpit Length	DC—Deep Condition	JBCO—Jamaican Black Castor Oil
BSL—Bra Strap Length	Dusting—Light Trim. Cutting only 1/8 to 1/4 of an inch	EVOO—Extra Virgin Olive Oil
MBL—Mid-back Length	Stretching—Prolonging the Time Between Relaxers	EVCO—Extra Virgin Coconut Oil
WSL—Waist-length Hair	Texlaxing—Underprocessed Relaxing on Purpose	
NG—New Growth		
BC—Big Chop		

Slip—Hair that a comb or fingers can glide through with relative ease.

More Hair-typing Systems

LOIS Hair-typing Method

The LOIS hair-typing method uses three characteristics to determine your hair type:

- *Pattern* (hair can be a combination, like OS or LS)

    — *L* = Bend
    — *O* = Curl
    — *I* = Straight
    — *S* = Wave

- *Strand size*—thick, medium, or thin (compare to sewing thread)
- *Texture*—thready, wiry, cottony, spongy, and silky (high or low shine or sheen, frizz factor)

The 'Curly Girl' Hair-typing Method

- *Corkscrew curls:* lots of small spirals with high tendency to frizz. Looks thick but actually lots of very fine hair strands. Tends to absorb a lot of water and tangles at the nape of the neck. Spring factor: 9-12 inches.
- *S-wavy hair:* looks shiny and straight without much effort. Slight bend at the ends of the hair and takes more effort to get the waves. Spring factor: 1-2 inches.
- *Wavy hair:* initially straight until around puberty but now starts to form waves once wet. Looks flat at the crown area and can look messy easily. 'Halo frizz' or frizzy ends with humidity and tends to dryness on the ends. Hair tends to look quite straight in the winter months. Spring factor: 2-4 inches.
- *Botticelli curls:* range of curls with looser, soft 'S' shape that seems to be pulled down as the hair gets longer. Spring factor: 5-8 inches.
- *Fractal or zigzag curls:* tiny spirals or step-like pattern on close inspection of strands. Very dry and needs very gentle

handling. Hairline may recede with tight pulling styles. Spring factor: 9-16 inches.

- *Cherub curls:* fine curl spirals that are very lightweight and fragile. Curly hair since childhood and seems to take a long time to grow. Spring factor: 5-10 inches.
- *Corkicelli curls*: curl pattern varies throughout hair, and hair tends to dryness and frizz if not properly moisturised. Length changes with humidity. Spring factor: 5-10 inches.

Curly girl hair type source: http://www.britishcurlies.co.uk/articles/categories/category/curl_types/

Clays and Hair Care

Bentonite Clay

Bentonite clay is an odourless, creamy-grey-coloured powder. It has a very fine, velvety texture in its dry state. Add water to make a grey paste-like mask.

Constituents:

Silica—61.4 per cent
Aluminium—18.1 per cent
Iron—3.5 per cent
Sodium—2.3 per cent
Magnesium—1.7 per cent
Calcium—0.04 per cent
Titanium—0.02 per cent
Potassium—0.01 per cent
Moisture—7.8 per cent
pH—8.3-9.1

Claims:

It is professed to attract dirt and toxins, thereby being a good cleansing agent. It can be used on hair as an alternative to a clarifying shampoo. On the face, it is often used as a purifying facial. It is also believed to be an intestinal detoxifying agent that has been used around the world for centuries.

How to use as a hair mask:

1. Use 60-100g of Bentonite clay. If your hair is longer or shorter than shoulder length, you will need more or less, respectively.
2. Add apple cider vinegar or water in small amounts and stir to mix. It should form a paste-like consistency. 'It will be lu+mpy—you've been warned!'
3. Stir 30 ml of aloe vera juice into the mix. 'This makes it smoother.'

4. Mix well to get rid of lumps.
5. Apply to your hair in sections and cover with a plastic cap for 20-30 minutes.
6. Rinse well.

Rhassoul Clay

This polished brown rock is quarry-mined from the Atlas Mountains of Eastern Morocco. It is sun-dried and then milled to make silkier, smoother texture.

Constituents:

Silica—58 per cent
Magnesium—25.2 per cent
Aluminium—2.47 per cent
Iron—0.64 per cent
Sodium—2.3 per cent
Calcium—2.34 per cent
Moisture—<8 per cent

Claims:

It has been used in Ancient Rome and Egypt as a soap, shampoo, and skin conditioner. Improves skin elasticity, clarity, and firmness and removes dead skin cell, thereby improving smoothness.

How to use rhassoul clay as a hair mask:

1. Mix 2 tablespoons with lukewarm water (more if needed—I use 60 g = 4 tbsp) to form a paste.
2. Apply to hair from roots to tips.
3. Leave on for 20-30 minutes with a shower cap over it.
4. Wash out thoroughly with warm or hot water.
   Add honey or aloe vera juice to increase the moisturising benefits.

Index

Made in the USA
Middletown, DE
29 October 2018